ORISHAS OF TRINIDAD

MONIQUE JOINER SIEDLAK

Oshun
Publications

ISBN: 978-1-950378-28-9

Publisher:

OshunPublications, LLC

Cover Design by MJS

Cover Image by Depositphotos

Books in Series

African Spirituality Beliefs and Practices
  Hoodoo
  Seven African Powers: The Orishas
  Cooking for the Orishas
  Lucumi: The Ways of Santeria
  Voodoo of Louisiana
  Haitian Vodou

Want to learn about African Magic, Wicca, or even Reiki while cleaning your home, exercising, or driving to work? I know it's tough these days to simply find the time to relax and curl up with a good book. This is why I'm delighted to share that I have books available in audiobook format.

Best of all, you can get the audiobook version of this book or any other book by me for free as part of a 30-day Audible trial.

Members get free audiobooks every month and exclusive discounts. It's an excellent way to explore and determine if audiobook learning works for you.

If you're not satisfied, you can cancel anytime within the trial period. You won't be charged, and you can still keep your book. To choose your free audiobook, visit:

www.mojosiedlak.com/free-audiobooks

WANT UPDATES,
FREEBIES & GIVEAWAYS?!
MONIQUE JOINER SIEDLAK
THE
ORISHAS
JOIN MY
NEWSLETTER!
mojosiedlak.com/newsletter-signup

Contents

ONE

The History of Trinidad and Tobago

The Republic of Trinidad and Tobago is a Caribbean country that consists of two main islands (Trinidad and Tobago) and a few smaller islands. But the territories of Trinidad and Tobago were not always united. Until 1888, they were separate regions, each with their own history and culture.

Early History of Trinidad

Trinidad, the larger of the two islands, was initially inhabited by the Arawak Amerindians and Carib Indians, who called it Iere (the land of the hummingbird). However, in 1498 Christopher Columbus reached the island in his third voyage. He claimed it for the Spanish Crown, renaming it La Isla de la Trinidad (the island of the Holy Trinity). Initially, the Spanish did not pay too much attention to the island as it lacked gold, the precious mineral that they so desperately desired. But that soon changed once Spain established its capital at San José in 1592, and the Spanish began enslaving the native people of Trinidad. The island did not have precious minerals, but it had tobacco and cocoa. It did not take much for plantations to be put into place and for other nations to see Trinidad's potential. The French brought West African slaves to help keep the estates running, and they assisted the Spanish in developing Trinidad.

In 1797, the British took over, and Trinidad became an official British colony in 1802. The British continued to develop Trinidad's plantation economy and slave-based society, abandoning the failed cocoa plantations in favor of sugar crops. But the plantation system was doomed to fail as the slave trade was prohibited, and the slaves gained emancipation in 1834. The now-freed West Africans abandoned Trinidad, forcing the British to bring in immigrants from India, Madeira, and China to work on the plantations and serve the colony. These immigrants were brought to Trinidad on short work contracts, which allowed them to return home after completion or buy land and settle on the island. This labor system remained in place until 1927 (almost 100 years), and it brought the cultivation of rice to the Caribbean island.

The Beginnings for Tobago

The name Tobago comes from the Carib word tavaco, which refers to the pipe that natives used to smoke tobacco. These natives were Amerindians and Caribs, much like Trinidad. Tobago was claimed by Columbus in 1498, but it was not colonized until 1628, most likely because the smaller island was not seen as a point of interest. When Charles the First of England attempted to give the island to the Earl of Pembroke, a world-wide feud for Tobago began. Suddenly, a handful of nations were interested in colonizing the small Caribbean island.

First, in 1632, Dutch settlers took the island by force, slaughtering all the natives. Then, between 1650 and 1814, Tobago changed ownership multiple times, so much so that to this day, it's still the most disputed Caribbean territory in history. Louis XIV of France declared Cornelius Lampsius the owner of Tobago. Yet, it was then claimed by the Duke of Courtland, followed by London merchants, Dutch, and even modern-day Latvians. In 1704, in an attempt to silence the conflicts between nations, Tobago was declared neutral territory. But that made the island vulnerable in the face of pirate occupation, which wasted no time in making Tobago their base. In 1763, the Treaty of Paris offered the British Crown ownership of Tobago.

As a British Colony, plantations of sugar, cotton, and indigo were established, and slave labor was booming. For two decades, the British were in control, but in 1781, the French captured back the island. The ownership of Tobago went back and forth between the British and the French until 1814 when it went back to being a British colony. All throughout this war over ownership, Tobago remained a prosperous territory. However, with the abolition of slavery, the island's economy slowly crumbled. Riots, extreme weather conditions, and the overall decline of the sugar prices only worsened the situation. Even so, the British managed to keep the rum production going, which was the last industry to dramatically fail. In 1884, the London firm that handled the plantations' finances went bankrupt, and the plantation owners left Tobago, leaving everything behind.

With the economy in shambles, Tobago was no longer viable as a stand-alone colony. In 1889, it joined Trinidad, becoming a dual-island British colony.

The Republic of Trinidad and Tobago

When the two territories were amalgamated, Tobago adopted the laws and constitution of Trinidad. Also, the islands' revenues were merged, annulling Tobago's debt. In the 1920s, trade unions started to pop up, and the people of Trinidad and Tobago began pushing for independence and democracy. A new constitution was adopted (both islands still used the Spanish law), which gave Trinidad the right to electoral representation for the first time in its history as a colony. But for someone to be eligible, there were many qualifications, such as ones for properties and language. From 25 members chosen by the people of Trinidad, only 7 met the requirements and were elected. The people were not happy, and they continued to demand the right to express their political views. After years of protests, in 1946, all adults had the right to vote.

In 1950, further changes to the constitution were made, so 18 legislative council members out of 26 were elected by the people. It instituted a policy-making council made of 9 people (out of which, 5 were selected by the legislative assembly), and it put in place a ministerial system, albeit a rudimentary one. This ministerial system would go on to become a cabinet, elected from members of the legislative council. This cabinet would gain the power to influence the Governor's decision, who was forced by the law to heed the cabinet's advice. Trinidad and Tobago's desire for autonomy kept growing.

The 1956 elections saw the People's National Movement (PNM) being the majority. This political party, led by Dr. Eric Williams, an Oxford graduate, sought to institute self-government. In 1958, Trinidad and Tobago co-founded the Federation of the West Indies, which had the goal of gaining independence as a country. Constitutional talks with the United Kingdom slowly paid off. Trinidad and Tobago now had internal self-government, a nominated Senate, and an elected House of Representatives. When the PNM won again in the 1961 elections, this new constitution was implemented. Jamaica withdrew from the Federation, and Trinidad and Tobago shortly followed, seeking to gain its own independence.

Meanwhile, the people expressed their frustration at the remains of colonial society that plagued the islands. The Black Power movement gained traction, and mutinies and riots threatened to destroy the colony from within. It did not help that the economy was in shambles. However, the political crisis ended up strengthening the national identity of the Trinidad and Tobago people. And in 1970, a lucky discovery of a valuable resource (oil) saved the colony from bankruptcy, bringing instant prosperity.

More constitutional talks with the United Kingdom ensued, and a constitution was drafted. Finally, in 1962 Trinidad and Tobago became independent, followed by the country becoming a republic of the Commonwealth in 1976.

A Time of Political Unrest

The PNM had a long run, and it was perceived in a favorable light. However, that changed in the 1980s, when the oil prices reached an all-time low, and recession hit. The PNM was accused of corruption, and in the 1986 elections, it lost to the National Alliance of Reconstruction (NAR) led by Robinson. But his alliance was shaky, and soon enough, the United Labor Front left the NAR and formed the United National Congress (UNC). Corruption bloomed in these times of political unrest, mostly due to drug-related trials.

In 1990, a minority Muslim faction attempted a coup. They stormed the parliament and took Robinson, along with 44 other members, hostage. The hostage situation lasted for 5 days, during which the country was in a crisis state. The poor areas of the capital suffered the most, with looting and violence reaching an all-time peak. Although the hostages were released, and the coup failed, the NAR government never recovered. PNM took over again in 1991, under Patrick Manning, a short-lived victory. In 1995, the UNC government came to power under Basdeo Panday (the first prime minister of Indian descent), strengthened by friction in the PNM.

The UNC held on to power until 2002 when Manning won the elections, putting the PNM back as the ruling government. Corruption scandals led to Manning losing the 2010 elections and saw a coalition of the UNC. The Congress of the People (COP) winning the election. Kamla Persad-Bissessar, the leader of COP, became the first female prime minister. Corruption allegations sparked again, and the PNM, under Keith Rowley, won the 2015 elections.

A Troubled Nation

If there is something to learn from Trinidad and Tobago's

history, it is that the country had it rough from the very beginning. The dual-island Republic was plagued by conflicts and battles for power, which seldom had the people's best interest at heart. From slave labor to political injustice, and the fluctuating economic crisis, the nation of Trinidad and Tobago had little to turn to for hope and reassurance. Many found their comfort in religion and traditions, which is why old beliefs survived the troubling times.

This book will focus on the importance of religion for the people of Trinidad and Tobago and how it allowed them to survive as a nation.

TWO

Roots of the Religion

The colonial era of Trinidad and Tobago had a significant influence on the religious beliefs of the native people. The indigenous population was relatively wiped out, and the islands were repopulated by African slaves and laborers brought from Asian countries to work the land (once the slave trade was banned). So, we can't speak of a native religion of the people but instead of the various religious beliefs that were introduced to the Caribbean country by its different owners.

How It Was Spread

During the Spanish colonial rule, the official religion of the country was Roman Catholicism. This religious belief was also strengthened by French and Haitian immigrants who ended up on the islands during the revolutions. During British rule, Anglicanism and Protestantism gained traction. Indian immigrants brought Hinduism and Muslim religions (both Sunni and Shia Muslims), further diversifying the religious pool of Trinidad and Tobago.

Some African people brought to the islands accepted Christianity, but most held on to their own beliefs. African religious sects present in Trinidad and Tobago include Shango or the Orisha faith (derived from the West African Yoruba religion), and Spiritual Baptists (a mixture between traditional African beliefs and Protestantism).

Out of all the diverse nations that brought their religious beliefs to Trinidad and Tobago, the African people were the most persecuted. This is because their celebrations and offerings were frequently mistaken for dark magic and satanic rituals.

Hiding from Persecution

When African people were shipped to the Caribbean Sea, they were forced to give up on their culture, language, and spiritual beliefs. The plantation owners feared the mystical power of their slaves. They feared it so much that they even banned them from using their ritual drums, and they outlawed their gods and goddesses. However, the African people clung to their beliefs, and to hide their religious practices from the white men, they disguised them under the veil of Catholicism. It wasn't something difficult to do, as African gods known as orishas are very similar to Catholic Saints. Orishas act as intermediaries between the people and the Supreme Deity, and the African people soon learned to perform their rituals and celebrations using imagery of the Catholic Church. The plantation owners did not care if their slaves wore amulets, and they rarely grew suspicious of their interest in herbs.

This disguise of beliefs kept the people safe, and the plantation owners at ease. Also, it allowed the African people to hold on to their traditions and spiritual heritage, a small but essential comfort in times of hardship and abuse.

Religion Today

In the 20s, Hinduism grew in significance alongside various fundamentalists, such as Evangelical churches and Pentecostals. In the early 21st century, the majority of people were Protestant, with Catholic and Hindu completing the top 3 most practiced religions of Trinidad and Tobago. Other beliefs, such as Muslim and Jehovah's Witness, also have plenty of followers. Still, a significant number of people fall under the category of other/unknown religions. The word "unknown" refers to the African-based faiths, known as Orisha in Trinidad and Tobago. Although Orisha religions are quite prevalent, Christian Protestants see them as demonic. This is why, decades after the colonial era, people are forced to practice their religious beliefs in secrecy. Still, out of fear of being shunned by their communities.

Nonetheless, the Orisha religion has a certain degree of popularity. The Orisha priests are open to offering consultation to people in need. Often by providing the visitor with an amulet or charm designed to bring good fortune (even political figures are known to visit such priests when the election season approaches). Many people join the religion to get help for daily problems, such as employment and relationships. Other people find refuge in the Orisha faith after traumatic events.

Trinidad and Tobago are one of the few countries in which the public perception of these African-based religions is almost entirely negative. With Orisha, followers and Spiritual Baptists have seen as pagans despite the religions' popularity.

THREE

The Shango Religion

The Shango religion in Trinidad and Tobago can be traced back to the middle 19th century. It is based on the worship of Yoruba gods known as orishas (which is why this belief is also known as Orisha religion). The modern inhabitants of the island country are the descendants of the African people who were transferred to work the land. These slaves brought their traditional rites and beliefs into the New World, remaining faithful to their Yoruba ethnicity.

Because persecution was a real threat for the African people, they were forced to adapt their religious beliefs to those of their masters to hold on to their spiritual heritage. The Shango belief has as a centerpiece the concepts and religious practices of the Yoruba cult. Still, it also encompasses elements from Catholic rituals and Hindu traditions. So, the Yorubas of Trinidad amalgamated their orishas with the saints of the Catholic Church, and they remained faithful to their African culture.

The modern-day worshippers of the Shango religion celebrate the major gods of the Yoruba pantheon, although under some different names. Yemoja, the mother goddess of the Yoruba people, became Ajajà o Mama Loatlè, "the mother of all nations," to the Orisha worshippers in Trinidad and Tobago. Obatala, the orisha that made the Earth inhabitable for people and created the first humans, is known as two individual entities, Batala and Lyamba, by the Shango practitioners. Olorun remains the supreme deity of the Orisha people, but a distant one who is seldom worshipped. The principal deity of the Yoruba people in Trinidad and Tobago is Shango, the orisha of thunder.

Shango the Orisha

Shango is the warrior deity of justice, dance, music, and masculinity. For the Yoruba people, he represents wealth, intelligence, the joy of life, and the special relationship between the people and the afterworld. Perhaps the people feel so close to the deity of thunder because they believe he was once human. He was not any random individual but an important king, Alafin, the 4th ruler of Oyo (a historic Yoruba city). Shango lived in a special time of Yoruba history when the people had lost their connection with the orishas. Olorun, the supreme deity, had sent Shango to rearrange society and help the townspeople learn how to live their lives to become one with the ancestral spirit.

However, after Shango became king, the people began to resent him. They believed he was too strict and reckless. Tales speak of his fascination for magical powers and how he would summon thunderstorms that wreaked havoc and killed innocent people. But he is also credited for inventing battle formation and extending the Yoruba Empire to new lands. He was loved and respected as a warrior king but feared for his experiments with magic powder. In the end, the townspeople wished he would be replaced. The problem was that in those times, the only method in which a king could be removed was for him to die.

When Shango became aware of the heinous plot that awaited him, he ran away and hid in a forest. There he ended up taking his own life. Shango's enemies celebrated his demise and belittled him for his cowardice. Then, out of nowhere, lightning struck the houses of Shango's enemies, and powerful thunderstorms destroyed half of Oyo. That's when the people understood that Shango was reborn as an orisha, a deity of thunder, and they began to worship him to escape his rage. All the myths and legends portray Shango as destructive but creative, capricious, magical, and an orisha of morality. He represents the unpredictability and violence of the divine power, which is why he is often celebrated through dance.

Something that you should know about orishas is that they are not seen as perfect. The Yoruba people believe that their deities resemble humans, meaning that they have both positive and negative characteristics. A kind God can, at the flip of a switch, become violent. A deity of mischief can aid people in hard periods of their lives. The Yoruba don't have deities that are just pure evil, which is why they don't have an equivalent for the Christian Devil. When an orisha is of questionable character, his or her purpose is ultimately positive, or he/she represents the necessary chaos that allows for good and order to exist. That's why Shango is a complex being, with good and bad characteristics. He is celebrated for both his strengths and his flaws. It is his imperfections make him more approachable and close to his people.

Shango's Worship

During the persecution days, Shango was worshipped under the guise of Saint Barbara.

Shango's symbols are the oshe, the double-headed ax, which represents lightning, and the bata drum that Shango uses to create thunder. During festivals, a dancer holds an oshe and moves to the rhythm of the bata drums. The dance moves are violent, warrior-like, and filled with threatening gestures but also mixed in with serene moments in which the dancer turns the ax to himself.

Shango's sacred number is 6, and its multiples and his colors are red and white. His celebrated day of the week is

Saturday. On this day, it is customary to bring an offering to the orisha of thunder. It may seem strange, but most Yoruba deities have particular numbers, colors, and days of the week assigned to them. It is because the Yoruba people see messages and symbols in the day to day things.

Altars dedicated to Shango are usually decorated with cedar tools, especially weapons (swords, axes, maces, sabers) and music instruments (drums and maracas). His worshippers wear red and white garments and unique traditional necklaces called elekes made of white and red beads. Shango's sacrificial animals are sheep, roosters, doves, Guinea hens, rams, and turtles. His favorite offerings include red wine, bananas, gumbo, green milk, palm oil, and pumpkins.

For someone to become a member of the Shango cult, he/she needs to go through an initiation phase, in which they receive certain powers. The initiation consists of the candidate wandering into a forest for some time, at the end of which, they receive a symbolic object considered to be sacred to Shango. This object signifies the power they receive because the Orisha followers believe in the will of the deities. The members are hierarchized based on the powers they received during initiation. All of the worshippers take part in the Shango ritual of Trinidad, where they dance around a central pole and sing hymns. Nowadays, the tradition of ritual music known as shouting has regained popularity after decades of it being prohibited.

The places of worship in the Shango religion combine elements from the Catholic cult with traditional African elements. From Catholic churches, they borrowed the altar, the pulpit of the preacher, the Bible, and the candles. The most notable African aspect is the central pole (known as the Poteau-mitan), which is adopted by a wide variety of African-inspired religions, such as Voodoo and Candomblé.

The clergy is hierarchized in a very organized system. There is a preacher who interprets the Bible from the Yoruba point of view. Teachers explain the dreams of believers, helping them find their path in life. Leaders have a role in baptizing new members, another tradition taken from the Catholic cult. Doctors use traditional medicine and special incantations to heal the sick. Prophets have the power to see the future and make divinations (they can tell someone's destiny). And last but not least, some nurses take on the role of priestesses.

Role in the People's Lives

The people of Trinidad and Tobago are still very attached to their traditional ways and their belief in the orishas. Some celebrate their deities in the privacy of their homes, while others publicly announce their spiritual view to help and guide others.

True Orisha worshipers live their life in concordance with the old Yoruba traditions. They hope to do enough good to end up in the realm of eternal happiness and become one with the Supreme Ruler Olorun. They present offerings to their orishas in hopes of appeasing them and gaining prosperity. And, most importantly, they hold on to traditions to honor their heritage and celebrate their differences. The worship of orishas is about communities helping one another and enjoying life, which makes it a significant part of the lives of people from Trinidad and Tobago.

FOUR

Obeah

Obeah is a system of healing and spiritual practices that was developed by the African slaves who were brought to the West Indies. It is similar to other African-inspired religious practices, such as Vodou and Hoodoo. It consists of healing rituals, communication with the spirits of the dead, spell-casting, shamanism, and other occult abilities. However, it is said out of all the spiritual practices from the African world, Obeah is the most feared and dreaded. Until recently, it was punishable by imprisonment or flogging in Trinidad and Tobago.

The Origins of Obeah

Obeah was handed down through the centuries by word of mouth, and it is hard to pinpoint where it originated. Some believe that the word "Obeah" came along with the African slaves who inhabited the Caribbean countries, dating back to the colonial era. Others believe that Obeah refers to an ancient, secret order that had a wide variety of occult powers that went beyond those of modern shamans and spell-casters.

The general theory is that Obeah comes from the Akan people. This West African tribe can trace back its history to the year 1076. Thus, it isn't a coincidence that the first use of the term Obeah in colonial literature comes from an alleged

Akan woman, Nanny of the Maroons. This old witch defeated the British in 1739. Nanny, as a character, is described as a bloodthirsty rebel, who possessed fearful spiritual powers, such as the ability to catch bullets with her bare hands and necromancy. Tacky's Rebellion was an uprising of the Akan slaves that took place in 1760. It was said to be aided by an Obeah practitioner, who gave them potions that protected the slaves from bullets and gave them courage. From the 1780s, there are references to Obiu-women, who are wise women that could speak to the spirits of the dead and who had otherworldly healing powers. So, the general consensus on Obeah at the time was that its practitioners dabbled in the occult but also had healing abilities that they would use on kind masters.

However, soon, Obeah became a source of anxiety and fear for plantation owners. The amulets and packets of herbs that the slaves wore made the white men paranoid of being poisoned. Many women were accused of trying to poison their masters, and in 1818, a law forbidding Obeah passed. Poison of any type was banned alongside noxious fumes and any harmful herbal mixtures. That did not stop some slaves from harvesting arsenic beans in their huts or practicing rituals that placed curses on others. Once someone was under such a curse, there was no saving them. European medicines were worthless in the face of the powerful Obi-men and Obi-women. In the plantation era, the most popular Obeah curse was "shadow-catching," which consisted of "stealing" a person's shadow. This practice gave the Obi-man the power to bring forth the person's death. The unfortunate victims would die without having any physical symptoms, and convictions were impossible to make. Who would be such a fool to risk angering an Obi-man?

African Shamanism

Obeah is perhaps the most obscure African tradition of sorcery, as it is veiled in secrecy. Even the word "obeah" means secrecy, as a testament to the religion's character. We can describe Obeah as an occult power used for witchcraft, magical practices, and communication with the undead and the gods. An Obi-man is seen as a hybrid between a sorcerer, a root doctor, an occult spiritual, a healer, and a Voodoo priest. Obeah is a source of power, making the Obi-men strong magicians who can use any occult system without fearing the wrath of the orishas.

Obeah has many elements of shamanism, as it uses techniques of gaining knowledge and developing worshipping practices, but it is most similar to witchcraft. In Trinidad and Tobago, Obeah is blended with Hinduism, Christianity, and the Muslim faith. It is not uncommon for Obi-men to use the Quran or Bible to summon demons or angels. But, in the dual-island country, the most popular manifestation of Obeah is that blended with the Orisha faith (both the Christian Orisha and the more traditional Baptist Orisha). Because Obeah is seen as a source of power, it can be easily adapted into other spiritual beliefs.

The Obi-man

The title of Obi-man or Obi-woman is given to a person that practices Obeah related to the worship of Orishas. These specialists of the dark arts usually live secluded from their communities in remote areas where they can practice their magic. Their spells and practices are often connected to the dead. Obi-men worship the orisha called Bones, the ruler of death, which borrows elements from the Buddhist deity Mara and the Vodou god Ghouede. Bones is worshipped alongside his female-side Oduda (The Black One), who also shares similarities with Hindu (Mother Kali) and Vodou (Mamman Brigitte) deities.

Although Obi-men are respected and feared, their lives are far from easy or perfect. They are antisocial beings who often live in inhumane spaces. They are thought to have the power to destroy anything or anyone that comes in their way. Obi-men preach the teaching of the Grimorium Verum and

Goetia, the alleged 6th and 7th books of Moses (biblically, Moses only wrote 5 books), which contain the witchcraft of the ancient Egyptians. Moses is frequently associated with Obeah, as he was believed to be a snake charmer. Ob, the Egyptian word for snake, is believed to be the origin of the name Obeah.

Items associated with Obi-men are cat ears, jars of grave dirt, human hair, and herb mixtures. Obeah teaching and practices are not restricted by gender, age, or social status. Any Orisha follower can choose the path of Obeah if he or she feels ready to give up on their previous life. And of course, one can practice Obeah without becoming a fearful Obi-man. The reason why Obeah is accepted as something real is that its practitioners have an exceptional knowledge about herbal medicine. Their teas, broths, and berry mixtures are known to cure ailments that modern pills had no effect on. On the flip-side, the poisons and curses of an Obeah cannot be treated by the advances of modern medicine.

Potions, Hexes, and Remedies

An Obeah follower is known to own a "wish-bag" full of potions, charms, and poisons. If a person wishes for his affections to be returned, an Obeah can provide a potent love potion, a perfume that promises eternal love. Potions for fearfulness are popular among women, while virility brews are appreciated by men. With his or her occult powers, an Obeah has control of both the living and the dead. An Obeah can ensure that the harvest season will be prosperous, that a business becomes profitable, or that an enemy can no longer possess a threat.

But an Obeah can also ruin relationships or, for the proper price, kill off someone. An Obi-man has many tools up his sleeve when it comes to killing, the majority of which are more innovative than the good old poison. They can use contaminated water, rusty nails, poisonous spiders, and so on. For those who can't afford proper potions or spells, a kind Obi-man can sell curse recipes. Roasted breadfruit filled with dried herring is sure to ruin crops if left on an enemy's land. Dirt from an enemy's footprint can be gathered in a bag, salted, and used as a pin-cushion, to give them nasty sores. Tell-tale signs of hexing include weird items left on someone's porch: the head of a white rooster, a dead lizard placed in a match-box, a coin, a handkerchief. If any recipe or hex fails, the Obeah can simply claim that the person was not a true believer, as only faith can make the spells work.

Grave dirt, known as Jumbie dust among the African people, is said to have potent powers. If sprinkled in a place where an enemy walks barefoot, his legs will swell up, covered by sores. The fever could kill a man if he does not go to the root doctor for the appropriate cure. The only one who can heal the damage done by an Obeah is another, more powerful master of the magic, a stronger Obi-man. Stories speak of men that died in the course of a week from the nasty sores and the generalized infection and of plantation owners' daughters who barely escaped death with the help of a bush-doctor.

The recipes and incantations of Obeah are often held under a vow of secrecy. An Obi-man's greatest fear is for his spells to be redirected at him by a rival Obeah user who happened to get a hold on his incantations and rituals. But some traditional formulas have been recorded in books such as Titabeth, The Black Arts, and Pow-wows With a Lost Friend. These were recorded by an underground press. Common-knowledge formulas include the use of wild sea-onion to dangerously speed up one's pulse. Castor-oil beans to cause intestinal issues, and soursop leaves brewed in hot water result in a home-made sedative, which can be used for both good and bad.

An ancient remedy would imply the use of exotic ingredi-ents, such as rainwater, limes, olive bush, sage, guava, elder, honeysuckle, and other leaves, all steeped in the right combination for a set period. Candles were also used for different purposes, depending on their color. Red candles were used to improve someone's luck. Blue candles were lit for love spells, while yellow candles brought forth great power. Green candles were used to bring about prosperity and money, and the fearful black candle was used for hexes and destructive spells.

Famous Obeah

A famous Obi-man is Ezra Bailey, who allegedly vowed on his death bed to come back to life and take his family with him to the underworld on the ninth day. It's the ninth the day in which evil spirits leave the body, in traditional belief. Ezra had a history of "devil play" and was known to be a powerful Obeah. Soon after his death, his wife and children got sick, and no medicine or herbal mixture could cure them. They died before the ninth day, claimed by the hand of Ezra himself, the locals would say. And even after the deed was done, stories of Ezra walking at night, looking for another soul to recruit for his undead army, never ceased to pop up.

Ezra's daughter, Jestina, was the only one who did not die from illness because she, too, was a master of the dark arts. She studied the ways of Obeah in Trinidad and returned to her home to follow in her father's footsteps. However, not all stories of Jestina present her as on old hag fond of hexes. Accounts describe her as a sweet-looking old lady who had a day job at a hotel. Who also practiced her magic at night for whoever paid her. Unlike her father, Ezra, Jestina also dabbled in healing. She used intuitive psychology, which was veiled as prophetic dreams and visions. Jestina also applied Christian incantations, and old root remedies to treat otherwise incurable diseases.

Jestina's hut was full of ingredients needed for witchcraft. Leaves and roots rested in pockets, ready to be used at any time. Powdery herbal mixtures lay next to human ashes, hair, and jars of potent Jumbie. Traditional calabash bowls held animal goods, such as bones and teeth. Other peculiar items, including cat and dog skulls, eggshells, feathers, and playing cards were scattered about, waiting patiently for their time.

Whereas Ezra Bailey was seen as a devil worshiper, opinions on Jestina vary. Her peculiar talents made her an easy target when it came to assigning blame. If something terrible happened, or someone got sick, Jestina was the scapegoat. She was feared, hated, but also respected for her healing abilities. It's interesting to see that such a famous character as Jestina Bailey was schooled in Trinidad, proving it to be the capital of the Obeah users.

Supernatural Creatures

There are a handful of ghouls and monsters that, supposedly an Obeah user can summon at his or her will. A jumbie (zombie) is an evil spirit who borrows the body of people who died recently. This evil spirit is said to have the power to inhabit a living animal or human and force them to commit crimes. These "zombies" were also blamed for sudden deaths. These deaths are referred to as a "jumbie's thief" or a "touch from the grave." Other spirits that walk at night are known to shrink themselves or turn into stones. They get ready to attack an unsuspecting victim that sits on them, or they take on the form of pigs (runks) and block someone's path. The only means to get rid of a runk is to hit it, as long as you don't count your blows. If you do count your hits, the runk will attack you.

La Jablesse is a siren who lures men that come home late into the woods for love affairs to get them lost. They take on the appearance of attractive women, but they can be identified by their hooves, which make a distinctive noise when they walk. Such sirens are also known to hunt deserted coral reefs and lure sailors to their deaths with their songs.

The loup-garou is the African-equivalent of the werewolf. However, this creature also can turn into other creatures. This fearful creature is said to devour any living creature, except for twins since many African cults believe that twins have supernatural powers. There are two ways to defeat a loup-garou. You can either harm him (this will turn him back to his human form) or outsmart him. Loup-garous have the compulsion to count things; that's why people leave 99 grains of rice or corn outside their house. When he would reach the 99th, he would be sure that there has to be one more gain and would start the counting all over again in search of the missing 100th.

Now that I've mentioned the werewolf, this section would seem incomplete without its ancient rival, the vampire. The Obeah vampire is known as the soucouyan, a she-monster that feasts on the blood of young children. It is said that the soucouyan can hide under the guise of old ladies by day, and only at night, she sheds her human skin and goes for a hunt. She can be defeated by finding her human skin and salting it. The salt shrinks the skin, and when the vampire returns, it can no longer wear it and pose as a human.

Obeah in the Modern World

Obeah is not a religion, but it is a belief that provides answers for the unknown and offers straightforward explanations for failures. Obeah practitioners are seen as lowly people who prey on the weak and thrive from people's fears and fantasies. Even in our modern days, many laws prohibit the practice of this African cult, because it is too closely tied in with curses and misfortune.

In Trinidad and Tobago, Obeah includes an unusual practice known as Moko-Jumbie. The practitioners of this practice are healers who dress in colorful garments and take part in carnivals as stilt dancers, a very different portrayal compared to the classical Obi-men. We'll find out more about Moko-Jumbie in the next chapter.

FIVE

Spiritual and Healing Practices

The religions of Trinidad and Tobago are spiritual practices that influence all the cultural aspects of the beliefs, including healing. The healing traditions of the orisha people are a combination of native Arawak and Carib remedies and folk African roots medicine. In other words, healing is a big part of religion, giving it a mystical aura that fascinates (and sometimes terrifies) the outside world. The healing itself does not only refer to physical ailments but also to spiritual, emotional, and mental problems, giving it cultural importance that prevailed in times of hardship.

Traditional healing practices involve the use of herbs, prayer, meditation, rituals, spiritual ceremonies, and dances. Even today, shamanistic healers treat the body and soul of devotees by consulting their ancestors, performing exorcisms. They will engage in ritualism fire dances and preparing ancient herbal mixtures (although modern healers frequently send the patient to a doctor if needed). People outside the orisha religious system see the healing practices of the African-Caribbean people as dubious, dangerous, and harmful. A sense of fear is engraved into the psyche of the Western civilizations, which shows through in ritual healing related art, literature, and movies. The idea of black magic, blood offerings, and rituals brings grotesque images to the minds of the "civilized" population. However, if we chose to have an open mind and look beyond our misconceptions, we'll find that the Hollywoodian ritualic healer character is as far from the truth as it can be.

Health and Disease

The people who came to the Caribbean region brought along their concepts of health and disease, which were combined with those of the native residents. Two notable ideas are those of the hot-and-cold balance and spiritual healing (curing people with the help of spiritual assistance).

The hot-and-cold humoral balance refers to a simplistic concept that explains most ailments, an imbalance resulting in excessively hot or cold diseases. A tropical disease can be treated with a cold cure, while a cold illness can be cured with the use of a hot remedy. Examples of hot ailments include fever, sore throat, infections, skin problems (such as rashes and sores), menstrual issues (pain, heavy flow), and diarrhea. These hot conditions were treated with cold plants or bitter herbs. Categorized by their taste and the color of their flowers, cold plants were used to prepare cooling remedies. They would have a calming effect on rashes, measles, and other infections, and they were thought to have blood cleansing properties. These hot-and-cold herbal remedies were not localized to the Caribbean space but were also widely used by the Hindu and the Chinese people in relatively the same period as the African and native population of Trinidad and Tobago.

Spiritual healing practitioners always associated with physical diseases with underlying supernatural causes. They utilized herbs and plants to treat physical symptoms and rituals to find and cure the spiritual problems. Root-based remedies were accompanied by songs, dances, and communal ceremonies in which the devotees prayed to the spirits for the health of the individual. Initially, the term Obeah was used in reference to these bush doctors that took on the role of healers for their communities. Still, the name gained negative connotations during the colonial era. Even now, traditional African herbal remedies have a terrible reputation among the Western people, who have not given up on associating them with evil spells and witchcraft.

Spiritual Healing Elements

The earliest form of Caribbean spiritual healing is the Santos, a Catholic religious figure carved from wood and used in a wide variety of rituals. These reasonably small wood figurines served as objects of worship in the homes of the native and African population of Trinidad and Tobago and as fertility tokens for the fields. The Santos are representations of different saints or orishas. Each wood figure would have easily identifiable traits such as specific tools such as a staff, a weapon, a sack, etc. Also, with the Santos are very vibrant in color, they would maintain a personalized color palette, and each wooden figure adheres to the sacred color of each deity.

The Santos were renowned for their abilities to channel the spiritual energy of the orishas, and they were used for divination, fertility, and healing rituals. It is said that the Santos can be filled with the essence of the orisha, allowing for a person to call forth the spirit's power for healing and emotional comfort. The Santos was mostly used in poor communities that had no access to medical care services. Because the orisha religions adapted their deities to Catholic saints, the Santos quickly found their place in Orisha, Vodou, and Santería rituals. Right alongside dolls, bottles, and other items linked with healing properties.

African-derived therapeutic practices are plant-based, consisting of infusions, potions, concoctions, aromatics, root-doctoring, and other remedies for evil spells and hexes. These plant-based cures are often paired with folk art religious elements. Such a feature is the Vodou beaded flag, used to mark the start of a Vodou ceremony or ritual. The flag depicts an image of the orisha or of an item associated with the orisha, adhering to the spirit's personalized color theme and portrayal. The flags have an essential role in rituals, acting as a means of welcoming and summoning the orishas for spiritual possession sessions and private or communal healing ceremonies. The making of the flags is also attributed to the influence and inspiration of the orisha and by some is considered to be a healing experience. There are also Obeah flags, which serve a different purpose. These flags are standardized, meaning that they all have the same iconography - a red cross on a black background, and they are used as protection talismans against Obeah spells.

Colored beads on their own have great importance in Yoruba-inspired cultures, and they are used to decorate bottles and other altarpieces. The colors, patterns, and numbers of the beads are in concordance with the sacred code of the orisha followers, where spirits can be expressed through different elements of our environment. Beads are also used for necklaces, bracelets, and other amulets that believers wear for protection and prosperity. On the altars of orisha devotees, a constant element is dolls, made out of cloth or other materials. Cloth dolls are used as mediums to communicate with the world of the dead and especially with deceased ancestors. The dolls are said to be filled with spiritual energy when they are made, which is why they can prove helpful in healing ceremonies and rituals. Some of these dolls can be used to absorb negative energies or evil spirits that possess the owner. They receive the name of their owner, and they are buried in hopes to trick death and get rid of the evil energy. The patient is then cleansed with the use of a rooster (the animal walks over the ill person 3 times) to cure all ailments.

Spiritual Healing Practices

The spirits of the ancestors are a big deal in orisha healing practices. These spirits are said to guide a person through dreams or divination ceremonies, and they can vary from deceased family members to old slaves or ancient magic users. They are represented through the use of dolls, paintings, and other artistic mediums. Similarly, with the Vodou flags and cloth dolls, they become imbued with spiritual power, allowing them to be used in rituals. These representations of the ancestors work as a communication device to the spiritual guides. A person can ask for advice regarding health and spiritual issues. The spirits of the dead are sometimes controlled with pendants or spells to heal an ill individual. These healing ceremonies are public, and paintings depict them as being colorful and energetical.

A person that suffers from an unknown disease can visit a spiritual healer for guidance. The medium can communicate with the spirits and get information regarding the person's health condition. This communication is achieved by linking their souls to the orisha through prayer and invocation. Some healers get their spiritual insight by using cowry shells to practice old orisha rituals or by using drums to connect with specific orishas. Once the medium knows the ailment of the patient, he can use his hands to "pick up" the pain/problem. Some healers believe that they were chosen from birth to act as spiritual doctors, while others hear the orishas' call later in life. Healers have a vital role in the religious community since they act as a middleman between the human world and the supernatural realm.

Health problems that appear during pregnancies are cured during a specific ritual in which a medium is possessed by a spirit and offers the woman a special bundle filled with spiritual power. Animal sacrifices are often used in healing ceremonies. A priest would sacrifice an animal to the spirits in exchange for a person's health.

Herbal Remedies

Since I took the time to present so many aspects of spiritual healing, it would be a shame to not talk some more about the herbal remedies of the African-Caribbean people. It's quite interesting to see how they approach diseases and what natural elements they use to treat both simple and complex medical conditions.

Remedies for the Common Cold

There are over 42 plant species considered to do wonders for the symptoms of the common cold, such as shandilay (Leonotis nepetifolia). The plant's leaves are used to make a brew that can cure fever and coughs. For the cold fever, hot plants were used, from the likes of Bambusa vulgaris, a species of bamboo. Its plants were macerated to create a remedy, or water was stored in the tubes to infuse it with healing properties. Also, Pimenta racemosa, which tea from the plant's leaves stimulates immunity.

Cures for Bad Blood

The blood is considered a key element in traditional African-Caribbean medicine, and "bad blood" leads to skin issues, abnormalities of the eyes, and sexually transmitted diseases. Such health conditions were treated with blood purifiers that sought to cleanse the patient's bowels, kidneys, liver, and spleen. The most popular blood cleanser of the Trinidad people is the somewhat famous Aloe Vera plant, renowned worldwide for its medicinal purposes.

Remedies for Intestinal Worms

The traditional African-Caribbean healers believed that worms were located in a special pouch known as a worm bag. Some of these worms were associated with health benefits, such as better digestion. In contrast, others were recognized as parasites that drained the body's nutritional intake. For minor cases of intestinal worms, herbal remedies were prescribed for a short period to kill or "put the worm to sleep," so the patient can get rid of it more naturally. Plants like Portulaca oleracea and coconut were used for their laxative effects to "expel" the evil in, this case, the worm. A Cucurbita maximum, a species of squash, is frequently used in Trinidad and Tobago as a cure for intestinal parasites.

Herbal Treatments for Fertility Issues

Infertility is a major taboo in the Caribbean world where a man is often judged for his capacity to father many children. With that, a woman is valued for her role as a mother. Bois bandé loosely translates to potency wood, is an herbal aphrodisiac that is highly valued by the men of Trinidad and Tobago. At the same time, the kola nut plant (Cola nitida) is prized by women who face fertility issues.

Women's Health Remedies

Because fertility is essential for the Caribbean people, menstrual irregularities, and child-birth issues were taken very seriously. Senna occidentalis was used to regulate menstrual cycles, and bush teas made out of Aristolochia rugosa were used to cleanse the uterus after birth. Another critical issue was the familial planning methods. In the colonial era, when the African people were enslaved, the general consensus was to avoid pregnancy, as no woman wished to birth their children into slavery. Abortifacient potions were taken under the veil of "remedies to increase uterine flow," with the cinnamon tree plant (Cinnamomum Verum) being a frequent ingredient of such mixtures.

Herbal Treatments for Children

In traditional African-Caribbean medicine, strong herbal remedies were only used on adults. Children were given teas and brews made out of mild plants, such as spearmint (Mentha Viridis), to treat typical health issues such as fever and intestinal worms. Herbal baths with cashew tree extract (Anacardium occidentale) and other plants were also frequently used for infants and babies to boost their immunity and protect them against evil spirits. Some mothers would give their babies a sip of the bathwater to treat their intestinal issues, especially constipation.

Remedies for Chronic Lifestyle Diseases

Medical conditions, for instance, diabetes and hypertension, are on the rise in the Caribbean world. In Trinidad and Tobago, many diabetes sufferers use herbal remedies to treat symptoms correlated with the chronic disease, especially for the numbing sensation in their feet. The top picks are Aloe Vera and garlic plant extracts (Allium Sativum). Garlic is especially popular among people with hypertension.

Although the people of Trinidad and Tobago are quite keen on their traditional medicine, nowadays, many ancient remedies have been lost due to a somewhat lack of interest in the new generation and to the difficulty of procuring medicinal plants.

Moko Jumbie

Trinidad and Tobago have the rather unique practice of Moko Jumbie, a form of Obeah healing that was more openly accepted by the religious communities due to its celebratory and colorful character. A Moko Jumbie is a healer but also a performer. The word "Moko" means healer or diviner, and "jumbie" is a colloquial term for spirit or ghost. Moko is also the name of a giant-like African deity who could see evil approaching due to his towering height. That's why a Moko Jumbie practitioner walks and performs on stilts.

Stilt walking is practiced in many different cultures, and the Moko Jumbie of Trinidad and Tobago was brought to the Caribbean world by the West African slaves. The practitioners are known to be part of secret societies, and they have a unique role in ceremonies and rituals. The Moko Jumbies are masked. Their whole bodies are covered by garments, including brightly colored gloves, velvet jackets, a painted skirt, and feathery hats, to completely hide their identities. The gigantic masked totems of color resemble otherworldly spirits, and their carefully choreographed dances are both mesmerizing and eerie in nature.

The Moko Jumbies are seen as protectors, and their presence is considered mandatory in some religious ceremonies and in rituals of passage (the celebrations of children reaching maturity). Because they walk on stilts, the Moko Jumbies are believed to be able to see evil before it arrives at a village or household. This is why they act as guardians and spiritual protectors. Besides that, the colorful allure of the Moko Jumbies and their stilted dance is seen as a way of mocking the evil spirits, repelling them.

Once a cult figure of West Africa, the Moko Jumbie of Trinidad and Tobago is now more of a touristic attraction and carnival performer. The Moko Jumbies wear long pants to cover their stilts, and when asked where they come from, they theatrically recite their story. A Moko Jumbie would say that he walked all the way from the West Coast of Africa and over the Atlantic Ocean. He would also say that he is the spirit of Moko, the orisha of fate and vengeance, who managed to stand tall after centuries of torment. Unfortunately, the modern Moko Jumbie has little to nothing in common with the Moko of West Africa.

The Modern World

The traditional African Caribbean healing practices are on their way to becoming a part of the contemporary culture of Trinidad and Tobago, despite misconceptions regarding the "evil" nature of the African-inspired healing rituals and ceremonies. These healing practices serve the higher purpose of preserving the ancient knowledge of herbal medicine and the heritage of the African and native people of the Caribbean world.

The healers, shamans, root-doctors, and plant-experts are becoming guardians of ancient knowledge, allowing it to prevail in the modern days. They are widely respected by their communities for their multi-dimensional approach to healing because they consider mental, emotional, and spiritual ailments too. They have repeatedly shown to put the best interest of their patients first by recommending them to modern doctors whenever their health conditions require a Western approach. As a result of that, more and more people are open to trying traditional remedies. Thus, indirectly, they come into contact with the culture and beliefs of the Afro-Caribbean people.

SIX

Ajajà o Mama Loatlè

Yemoja is a primordial Yoruba goddess of rivers and oceans. She is one of the most worshipped orishas, with followers scattered all around the world from West Africa to the Americas, Trinidad, and Cuba. Yemoja is the ultimate mother figure, resembling the concept of the Christian Mary, the Mother of God. Her name in Yoruba translates to "Mother of Fish" (meaning that her children are so many that they can't be counted). Still, her followers often call her Ajajà o Mama Loatlè, meaning "The Mother of Everything." Just like many other orishas, Yemoja's cult and worship have adapted over time in response to her followers' needs and possibilities. However, her essence and role have remained the same. This allowed her to serve as a pillar of comfort and compassion for her followers, especially during the slave trade era.

Yemoja the Mother Deity

Yemoja is the undisputed orisha of water, and thus, she shares many attributes with the natural element. Water is seen as the source of all life, which makes the ground fertile and brings about prosperity. In association, Yemoja is an orisha of fertility who takes on the role of a mother for her people. She is portrayed as being caring, nurturing, and protective but also intelligent, rational, and fearful when needed. She is a guardian of the weak and innocent and a protector of those who works near water, such as sailors, fishermen, port workers, etc.

Yemoja is identified within all items related to water (shells, fishnets, miniature boats, and live fish) and with the color blue (peacock feathers, blue and white pottery, blue satin, or velvet, to emphasize her royal status, and the fluidity of water). In many cultures, she is associated with specific water bodies (specifically the river Ogun, with streams that have a sinuous trajectory and the water of life /amniotic fluid). She is often described as the mother goddess of all the orishas. Depending on each specific cult, this varies. Some of her followers believe her to be a hybrid between a human and a fish or a dark-skinned mermaid. In Trinidad and Tobago, she is celebrated as the goddess of saltwater and seas, which contradicts other religious cults that see her as an exclusive freshwater deity.

Yemoja's sacred number is 7 to represent the seven seas). She is frequently described as wearing 7 skirts of blue and white color or a flowy skirt with 7 seven blue and white layers. Her representation and worship are often assimilated with that of Olokun, the goddess of waters that assisted Olorun in creating the world. Olokun is seen as Yemoja's violent side, which she shows to whoever threatens her children. Olokun is known for her ominous powers that know no boundaries, her ruthlessness, and spite. Yemoja's motherly attributes are balanced by Olokun's fierceness. Thus, Yemoja is just like the waters, sometimes still and sometimes violent, beautiful, but destructive. When displeased, Yemoja is known to be stern and inflexible in her punishment. She doles out stomach aches, tuberculosis, or she can arrange for offenders to be dragged into the waters, never to be seen again.

Myths of Yemoja

Practitioners rely on myths and songs to remember the

lives of the orisha. However, these myths are often contradictory or different depending on the specific region in which they are popularized. Myths in traditional African culture change to better fit the needs of the people. Because the majority of these stories were passed down by word of mouth, one legend can have multiple variations. Myths of Yemoja make no exception. Some accounts place her among the primordial orishas that lived in Heaven alongside Olorun.

In contrast, others worship her as a human that ascended to divinity due to extraordinary deeds and supernatural abilities. She is frequently portrayed as a wife, co-wife, sister, or mother of various male orishas, including Shango, Ogun, Oshun, and Obatala. Her role changes depending on the culture and social norms of her followers. Keep all these aspects in mind as we explore a few stories of Yemoja.

An important and controversial myth of Yemoja is that of her becoming the mother of all the orishas. In this story, Yemoja is the daughter of Obatala and Odudua (an earth deity). She marries her brother Aganju (an orisha of the wild) and gives birth to Orungun. However, in a turn of fate, Orungun ends up falling in love with his mother. Blinded by a crazy passion, he confesses his feelings, which terrifies Yemoja. She blatantly refuses him, but he, a son of a wild deity, attacks her and forces himself onto her. Yemoja runs away in shame and anger about what has happened.

Orungun follows her and attempts to persuade her. In his enthusiasm, he tells her to accept him as her second, secret husband and argues that he could not live without her. As Orungun reached out to her and tried to seize her in his arms, Yemoja fell, turning into an enormous lagoon. From her body of water emerged numerous orishas such as Shango, Oya (a goddess of water), Orishako (the god of farming), Ogun (the god of war), and many others. At the site of Yemoja's demise, the town of Ife, the origin of all people, is said to have been built.

One legend of Yemoja serves as an origin story to the great Ogun River. In this story, Yemoja was a common woman who worked as a watermelon seed picker or meat seller to make her living. She marries the king of Oyo, Oranmiyan, with whom she gives birth to Shango. After some time, she left Oranmiyan and married the chief of the town, Saki, Okere. During an argument, Okere insults her breasts, and Yemoja attempts to flee. But Okere catches her and kills her on the spot. As a result, she turned into the Ogun River. Because of this myth, the Okere people hide their faces when they cross the Ogun River on their way to the city of Oyo.

Another similar story presents Yemoja as a beautiful woman who had an embarrassing secret: she was born with only one breast. That is why, despite her beauty and good nature, she remained unmarried and alone. Yemoja dreamed of having a husband and becoming a mother, so much so that she lamented out loud. As fate has it, the god of war Ogun happened to hear one of her laments, and he felt the unstoppable desire to marry her. He went to Yemoja and asked for her hand, but he prefaced his proposal with one condition: she could never make fun of his blood-shot eyes. Yemoja agreed and spoke of her own condition, which was for him to never touch her one breast. They married and led a happy life. They parented many children and kept their promises.

However, one fatidical, day Ogun got the idea to make a soup for Yemoja, to show his appreciation for her. But the god of war had no experience with working in the kitchen, and he dropped the soup pot, awaking Yemoja from her nap. She stormed in, angry and confused. In her anger, she forgot about her promise and made a snarky remark about Ogun's eyes. In return, he lost his temper and struck Yemoja down. Ogun regretted his actions immediately, as he cared deeply for his wife. He knelt down to her and stroked her breast in an attempt to comfort her, forgetting about his promise. Yemoja felt so ashamed of her physical defect that she transformed into water to escape Ogun's embrace. The god of war felt sad about losing her, but he concluded that love was not for him, and he went on to fight in many battles. The moral of this story is that Yemoja became an orisha to escape her hard life and leave behind her sadness and humiliation.

Other myths portray different sides of Yemoja. For example, in one legend, Yemoja uses her power of seduction to steal from the harvest deity's farmer her secret of planting sacred yams. Her motivation was to obtain the orisha's drums that her son Shango desired, showing that the kind mother would go above and beyond for her beloved children. Yemoja's sensuality is explored in many stories that are not for the faint of heart.

Yemoja, a Changing Concept

As I have mentioned before, Yemoja's myths and attributes changed alongside her people. Initially, she was a mother and a wife who did not bow down to the men in her life. Whenever she was abused or in danger, she turned herself into a river to escape her fate. She showed her independence and free will whenever she felt wronged, and she even could give birth to other deities without the help of a man. However, the Yemoja of the colonial era saw massive changes. She becomes a subordinate of the male figures in her life, namely her husbands or sons. Yemoja stoops down to lowly acts to fulfill her son's wishes, and she always aims to please Shango, Ogun, or Okere. From a pure mother figure, Yemoja changed into a seducer, a deceiver, a promiscuous woman who sought nothing but to fulfill her sexual desires. This shows how the role of the women in the society had changed. How they were seen as a force of corruption influenced by Catholic beliefs.

During the slave trade, Yemoja was associated with different saints (all maternal figures) to maintain her religious belief. In Latin America, she was correlated with the Virgin Mary, in Cuba; she was associated with the "Black Madonna" (the saint of Havana Bay). In Trinidad, she became known as being one with Saint Anne.

The most consistent aspect of her worship is her association with the colors white and blue. Her followers wear blue and white dresses, and traditional necklaces called ileke, which are made of blue and white beads. The ileke is often gifted and worn by pregnant women to protect their unborn child. Yemoja's symbols are the calabash and stones, which are placed on river banks or near water. They usually work as small shrines where people can bring offerings. Most of Yemoja's shrines and places of worship are near water bodies, and they are decorated with blue and white items or objects relating to the sea. Yemoja's favorite offerings include yam, ducks, fish, hens, goats, and mashed corn.

There is an annual autumn festival dedicated to the mother orisha. It is held in the town of Ayede, and the festival's purpose is to ask for Yemoja's favor in keeping the king healthy, the harvest abundant, and the women fertile. The major event of the celebration is the high priestess' ritual. She has to balance a sacred calabash or a statue of Yemoja on her head, like a crown, from the shrine to the king's palace without dropping it or uttering a word. Once she gets to the king, she turns away three times before allowing him to place his hands on her, symbolizing the transfer of Ashe (spiritual energy) and reinstating the importance of the king.

Yemoja's Importance

No matter how much her personality has changed, Yemoja remains the most important mother deity of the Orisha faith and the most beloved water orisha. The African people brought Yemoja with them to all the corners of the world where they were forcefully sent. They managed to change their perception of her to preserve her importance, and, in exchange, she became a symbol of hope, love, and comfort for the African slaves.

Even in our modern days, mothers seek out Yemoja's

protection, kings demand her acceptance, farmers pray to her for prosperity, and those in pain long for her comfort. Despite her role and mythology changing with times, Yemoja retained her core aspects. She is a protector, a healer, a nurturer, and a kind deity, the divine mother, the Ajajà o Mama Loatlè.

SEVEN

Olorun

Olorun is the all-knowing supreme deity of the West African people, who is accepted as the creator and leader of all orishas. Although the concept of Olorun is specific to the Yoruba people, one cannot worship orishas without recognizing that the Divine Ruler exists. Especially since orishas act as intermediaries between humans and Olorun.

The Concept of Olorun

Olorun is known under many names, such as Olofin-Orun (The Lord of Heavens), Olodumare (The Almighty), and Oba-Orun (The King of the Sky). This ruler of the heavens is a distant deity who does not meddle in the everyday lives of mortals. Olorun is often seen as a concept more than a deity. The absolute goal of an Orisha worshipper is to achieve the state of Olodumare, which means becoming one with the divine creator, Olorun. The West African people believe that all living things were born from Olorun's spiritual essence; thus, that's where they should return after death.

The fact that Olodumare is seen more as a concept than a deity explains why this divine creator is not limited by human concepts, such as gender or form. Olorun is genderless, and the pronoun "they" is used when referring to this deity.

Olorun is rarely depicted as having a human form. This also explains why Olorun is not worshipped or celebrated as openly as other Orisha through feasts and festivals. The divine creator is honored subtly, through the daily lives of their subjects. Orisha worshippers live their lives in a way designed to bring them closer to Olorun. One can become connected to the energy of the world through good deeds, showing great character, and always trying to become a better version of themselves. To put it simply, only good, kind individuals deserve to become one with Olorun. During which mean-spirited people end up in the Orun Apadi (the realm of Potsherds representing Hell).

We can say that Olorun is the last mentioned African deity but the most worshipped, as all acts lead to him, and all that exists is part of him.

Olorun, and the Myth of Creation

Olorun is an essential figure in the African creation myth but not a central one. According to legends, Olorun created the world alongside Olokun, the ruler of waters. Olorun made the heavens and its inhabitants, the orishas, and Olokun created a vast ocean. So the world at the beginning of the Universe was just a sky and a formless mass of water, and nothing more.

The orishas lived in the sky, alongside Olorun, in peace and harmony. They had a baobab tree that gave them everything they ever needed, from food to fancy garments and expensive ornaments. Olorun encouraged them to explore the heavens, but they were too content with their lives to even try. Only Obatala, a curious orisha, wished for something more. He had seen that the world below the sky was just a vast mass of ocean, empty and unfit for life, and he came up with an idea. Obatala wanted to create solid land, with forests and fields, so other creatures could thrive. Olorun appreciated the orisha's initiative to do something productive. It allowed him to descend to the watery world and create land.

That's how Obatala's mission started. With help from Orunmila, Olorun's eldest son, and the prophet orisha, Obatala began his preparations. He needed a chain made of gold to use as a ladder and descend from the heavens; sand; a palm nut; seeds, a white hen, and a black cat. To make the chain, Obatala asked for the orishas to give him their jewelry and ornaments, to which they obliged. The blacksmith melted those and created the links and a golden hook to put at the end of the chain. With the chain done, Obatala gathered sand in an empty snail shell and gathered all the ingredients he needed and started his descent. It took his 7 days to reach the ocean below, and poor Obatala had no clue what he was supposed to do with the peculiar elements from his pouch.

Then, Orunmila guided him once more. He told him to pour the sand into the waters and release the hen. The fowl got to work and scratched at the sand, creating islands of dry land in the process. Still clueless, Obatala reluctantly jumped from the chain and became the first being to walk on land (excluding the hen). He named the land Ife (the primordial city of the West African people), and he began exploring the place. In his path, he planted the seeds, which grew immediately, filling the land with luscious green. Obatala walked and walked with his cat companion, but he soon became thirsty and lonely. He stopped at a pond to quench his thirst but got distracted by his reflection. He got the idea to create an image of himself using the clay that lay at the edge of the pond.

In no time, Obatala created several perfect figures. Now, his thirst was worse than ever, s, he made the mistake of drinking palm wine, believing that it would energize him. However, the wine went right to his head, and he began creating incomplete figures, with missing limbs and weird features. With a foggy mind and a feeling of loneliness ever-growing, he asked Olorun to bring his clay people to life, to keep him company. Olorun obliged. The divine ruler created a huge fireball, which they sent to Ife to bake the clay men and dry off the lands. Then, Olorun blew his breath on the clay figures, bringing them to life. Obatala was grateful and remorseful. He felt ashamed for his mistake, but he vowed to protect and love his creations as they were. Olorun asked the other orishas to protect the people and listen to their prayers.

Olorun's role at the beginning of the world does not end there. With the lands and the humans created, all seem well, but, in Obatala's fervor to create the solid ground, he forgot to ask for permission from the goddess of the waters, Olokun. She was not happy with her kingdom being shrunk, and she sent the fury of the waters down on the poor citizens of Ife. Orunmila stepped in to save the humans, enraging the goddess even more. This time, she challenged Olorun to a weaving contest that would decide who was the most powerful god. Olokun was a master weaver, and her skill could not be matched even by the creator himself. However, Olorun figured out a way to win the contest without also participating. Olorun sent Agemo, the chameleon, to spy on Olokun and change his skin to match the pattern of her work. Olokun was humbled when she saw that even the ruler's messenger could match her skills. Defeated, she accepted Olorun as a supreme ruler, and she allowed the people to live in peace.

Symbolism

Olorun symbolizes the original creation, the goal of every Orisha followers' life, and the father of all. Even though Olorun does not have a physical form, there are elements in nature that are associated with the divine ruler. All white things, such as bones and clouds, are said to be linked with Olorun, and so is human consciousness. The West African people have a concept of "internal head," which is supposed to be ruled by the orishas and by Olorun.

The Orisha Worshippers Have Many Praise Names For Olorun:

Alabosunife (The Protector of the City of Ife) - this means that Olorun looks after all living beings from their source because the West African people believe that Ife is the origin of all life.

Alabosudaye (The Protector of the Earth) - this name shows that Olorun wishes for the best outcomes for the people and their planet. But the Divine ruler can see the bigger picture, unlike anyone else, which is why sometimes, the things that happen in the world baffle us. Olorun is known to work in mysterious ways and always with the best interest of humanity in mind.

Alaye (The One Who Lives) - this name refers to Olorun's immortality. Since Olorun is energy, they can't be destroyed, only altered. This is also a reference to the African belief in the reincarnation of the soul.

Elemi (The Owner of Breath) - Olorun is the one who gave life to Obatala's clay figures, making him the divine creator. In traditional belief, before birth, an individual's destiny is mapped out from start to finish, the body is created, and lastly, Olorun provides the soul.

Olojo Oni (The Owner of Today) - this name shows that no matter what orisha one chooses to worship, Olorun will always be the ruler of the world and the creator of each passing day.

Olorun is and always will be the most respected and influential deity for the Orisha worshipers.

EIGHT

Possession

The orishas of the West African cultures are the masters and patrons of old arts, such as farming, science, medicine, and divination. According to ancient myths, Orunmila, the prophet orisha, was asked by Olorun to stay on earth and live among humans to help and guide them throughout their lives. The act of humans receiving advice from orishas is known as divination, and this is a private practice. Spiritual possession functions on the same basis but in a social, communal environment, with an audience watching.

Manifesting an Orisha

Spiritual possession in African religions is seen as a means of honoring and communicating with supernatural beings (the orishas). They accept the deities because it allows the orisha to be present to the ceremonies. Possessions are often compared to riding a horse, the rider being the orisha. In this context, possession has a positive connotation, as it helps the possessed, allowing him to discover new sides of himself without the fear of being judged. It is common for a possessed individual to behave in weird and strange ways to do the bidding of the orisha. Possessions happen in controlled environments, and they are performed during religious ceremonies. The general belief is that a spiritual possession can bring benefits to the entire community, not just to the possessed individual because they generate Ashe or spiritual energy, from the orisha.

To be able to receive spiritual energy from the orisha, the people that take part in the ceremony need to achieve a trance state, which is done through dancing and specific drum rhythms. Each orisha has its designated drum, and particular drumming rhythms are associated with one particular orisha, so the community can connect with the orisha of their choice. The fast drumming induces a dream-state, and the simple dancing steps prepare the audience for spiritual possession. After the state of trance is achieved, the people begin to use the steps and dance moves that are associated with the orisha they wish to connect to.

Possession is manifested in different ways. Some people may have seizure-like states to show that a spirit has inhabited their bodies. Others dance in a weird fashion, make peculiar facial expressions, or become an entirely different person (personality-wise) and interact with the audience. Possessed people can speak in native African dialects, walk in strange ways, or even experience gender dysphoria. The experience can last from a few minutes to a couple of hours. This will depend on the type of ceremony, and the traditions of the people involved.

Being a Medium

Not anybody can become a "vessel" for the orishas. Mediums need to go through extensive training and have to manifest supernatural abilities from a young age. The first spiritual possession is described by many as being shocking, rough, and borderline traumatizing for the future medium. This supernatural experience is interpreted as a call of the orisha, for that person to become initiated. The initiation period can last for a couple of years, and it consists of training into becoming a suitable medium. A person learns how to call an orisha, how to control the will of the spirit, and how to end the session at will. For many African cults, spiritual possession is seen as both an honor and a spiritual obligation. In some Orisha beliefs, only a select few get to become mediums. In contrast, in others, the spiritual possession can be achieved by a broad group of believers.

Although most spiritual possessions happen in controlled environments, it is not unheard of for mediums to be contacted by the orishas at random times of the day. A medium that feels the call of the orisha would stumble in their walk or shake furiously. The members of the community know how to recognize the signs of possession, and they would immediately come to the aid of the medium. They would stay with the medium to care for his physical health. Remaining on the safe side, they would remove any objects that could be destroyed or could harm the medium (such as sharp tools, jewelry, glass items). As well as they would patiently wait for the orisha to make his/her wishes known. Every orisha has a specific temperament that influences the spiritual possession experience. Some are violent and take control immediately, while others take their time in assessing control over the medium.

Spiritual Possession in Different African Cults

Every African cult has its own understanding of spiritual possession and how it should be practiced. The Orisha belief of Trinidad and Tobago has elements of many cults, which is why I will take some time here to present the various interpretations of spiritual possession.

Candomblé

The Brazilian Candomblé is centered around orisha worship. They see the deities as forces of nature or energies, and they don't believe that an individual can be possessed by pure energy. That's why the Candomblé followers don't use the term spiritual possession but rather spiritual manifestation. Only a medium can control this energy that would make an average person collapse to the ground. A medium needs to train for several years to become a master in the arts of spiritual manifestation, and a medium in training is seen as a child that needs to learn the works of life. In Candomblé, the general belief is that a medium connects to three orishas at a time. As a result, a part of their energy always stays behind, like an echo. This residual energy is re-used in future possession sessions, making it easier for the orishas to take control.

So, rather than being possessed by an external force, the Candomblé medium suffers an internal transformation. The general consensus is that a medium is forever changed by his first interaction with the divine energies. The orisha is regarded as a part of a human's consciousness that shines through during the spiritual manifestation practice. Also, through this manifestation, the orisha, that the Candomblé people see as natural forces, receives a personality and becomes an individual, rather than energy. This belief explains why an orisha can have different characteristics and how it is possible for an orisha to be in connection with different mediums at a time. Each spiritual manifestation changes both the orisha and the human, creating a new, unique entity.

In Candomblé, the possessions usually happen in temples during religious festivities. The trance is induced with the use of the sacred drums, and the old Yoruba dialect is used to announce each orisha taking hold of the individual. The medium occupies a central position while the congregation dances in a concentric circle to channel their energies to the medium. After the possession occurs, the medium changes into garments that suit the orisha (with the specific colors and decorative elements), then the orisha takes the lead, providing general advice and guidance for the devotees. In the morning hours, the orisha reverts to a child state, characterized by play-fulness and obscene behaviors. This is a sign that the posses-sion has reached its conclusion, and soon, the orisha leaves.

The medium has no recollection of the events that happened during possession.

Vodou

In Vodou, spiritual possession is very theatrical. It is seen as a struggle or fight for control between the spirit and the medium. During ceremonies, the spirit of the medium leaves the body so the orisha can have full control. So, for Vodou followers, the vessel (medium) is no longer human during the possession, and the orisha can communicate with the audience and join them in celebrations (by feasting and drinking with them).

A Vodou medium is nothing more than a vehicle for the loa (spirit), and the presence of the spirit is seen as an answer to the community's prayers and requests. In Vodou's spiritual possessions, dance and animal sacrifices have a significant role. It is very common for the spirit to receive an animal offering of its liking, and dancing is used both to honor the orisha and to call forth his/her spirit. Similar to Candomblé, once a possession takes place, the medium is dressed in garments to fit the orisha's worship. He receives accessories and paraphernalia associated with the orisha (weapons, specific pieces of jewelry, etc.). In Vodou, playing cards and bones are also used to communicate with the loas, but for divination purposes, not public possessions.

A side note about Vodou's spiritual possession is that it has been linked with political actions, which is unique to this cult. Political characters have claimed to be possessed by a loa to gain the support of the masses. During the Vodou practice of zombification (the use of toxic substances that alter the state of mind) to empower their troops in times of war. Zombification has nothing to do with the orishas, but it is a cruel practice used to display power.

Santería

Santería worshippers believe that a person is linked from birth with a specific orisha, leading to a lifetime bond. This bond is confirmed in an initiation ceremony, which allows the orisha control over the mind of the medium. In a way, the person becomes an embodiment of the orisha. During possessions, the human spirit leaves the body and has no control over his actions or words. Although spiritual possession is mostly done by Santería priests, it is not uncommon for regular people to experience mounting (a reference to possession being like mounting a horse), which is a sign that a spirit calls to them to become initiates.

Spiritual possessions occur during religious festivities, and they resemble Candomblé sessions. In Santería, communication with the orisha can also be done through divination, which is private. Diloggun can be practiced by any priest, and it implies the use of coconut pieces or cowry shells as a means of communicating with the spirits. The coconut or shells are divided into pieces, and a number is chosen for a reading (the number depends on the orisha called since each spirit has its own sacred number). Chants and rituals are used to call the orisha and read his/her answers to the questions. Ifa divination can only be done by high priests, as it involves direct communication with Olorun. The rituals also use coconut pieces or shells, but the reading is done differently and repeated 8 times to ensure accuracy.

Umbanda

In the Umbanda religion, the spirits that take control of the medium are seen as individuals rather than energies. They can be spirits of African slaves, creole people from around the world, fishermen, gypsies, and so on. Each spirit has a specific vibration, which allows the medium to identify and summon it. The goal of these spirits is to offer their help to the community or the client, if the possession is private. The medium's appearance and demeanor changes to fit the spirit's personality. The Umbanda people believe that orishas are too powerful for a human body to handle, and only the orishas who have ascended from humans can be summoned through spiritual possession. This practice is, however, very rare, and the majority of spiritual possessions involve guiding spirits. These spirits, known as gufas, are seen as beings that are higher than humans but lesser than orishas, which makes them more approachable to mediums.

Possessions are accompanied by religious music (such as Ave Maria), and the session resembles that of divination, meaning that questions are used to gain advice from the ancient spirits. However, when orishas are involved, the ritual resembles that of the Candomblé religion.

Possession in Trinidad and Tobago

Possession is the only religious practice that follows the same rules and traditions both in Trinidad and in Tobago. That is because the islands have inhabitants that adhere to different religious cults despite the territories being recognized as one country.

Music is used to achieve a state of trance, and the possession itself resembles that of the Vodou religion, with several influences from the other African cults. The rituals take place in the capital of Trinidad and Tobago, Port of Spain, and animal rituals are used to honor and appease the loas.

NINE

Serving the Orishas

The Caribbean is full of a variety of religions, and Trinidad and Tobago are no exception. Many of the spiritual movements practiced on the island worship deities known as orishas. However, each religious cult has its own interpretation of the concept of divine spirits. These religions are known as Afro-Caribbean Creolized religions, and, depending on their core traditions and beliefs, they have different ways of understanding and serving the orishas.

Religions of Trinidad and Tobago

Creole religions appeared as a "creolization" of Catholicism during the colonial era, a process that assimilated native African deities and traditions into the Catholic cult. This allowed for Creole religions to fly under the radar of the plantation owners. Religions and spiritual beliefs vary from island to island, and it is very common for a West Indian country to be home to different Creole cults. In Trinidad and Tobago, we have a wide array of orisha-based beliefs, out of which, Santería, Vodou, Shango, and Spiritual Baptism are the most popular.

These religions have similarities and differences. They all

combine monotheistic and polytheistic elements, with them having one supreme god (Olorun) and other significant deities (the orishas). Spirits are seen as very important, and it is believed that they can influence the daily lives of believers through different means. Contact with the spirits is a significant point of Creole religions, and it can be done through divination and spiritual possessions (public ceremonies). Inanimate objects can also gain supernatural powers if they are significant to a specific orisha. Most African-inspired religions have a spiritual leader who can hold religious ceremonies and pass on the wisdom of the orishas to the community. Ritual dance and music are essential elements of orisha worship of all cults. They are often seen as ways to achieve a trance that allows for spiritual possession or communication with the deities. Another similarity is the air of secrecy and mysticism that surround each orisha cult of Trinidad and Tobago. Most devotees believe that their practices should be kept as guarded secrets, and there is a general reluctance to accept newcomers.

The differences make it so that every religion is unique in its own way. Most variations in beliefs and traditions come from the influences of the Creole religions. Santería, Shango, and Spiritual Baptism are heavily influenced by the West African Yoruba cult. At the same time, Vodou combines Yoruba traditions with other African religious practices. Another aspect that makes Vodou the odd one of the bunch is that its devotees delve in spellcasting and witchcraft (Obeah), during which the other Creole religions don't practice magic of any kind.

Now that we've seen what's the common ground for the African-inspired religions of Trinidad and Tobago, let's have a glance at each one of them and see how they chose to serve the orishas.

The Shango Cult
Since the Shango cult is the most symbolic Creole religion

of Trinidad and Tobago, it's fitting to put it at the head of the list. The Shango religion of Trinidad is based on the Yoruba Shango cult, dedicated to the West African deity of thunder and lightning. Still, it also includes several other orishas both from the Yoruba pantheon (such as Yemoja and Olorun) and from different religious beliefs such as Saint Gabriel and Mama Latay (Mother Earth). The ancient African deities are associated with Catholic saints, a practice that is common with most Creole religions. Some examples of orishas that are linked to Catholic saints are Yemoja and Saint Anne, Oya and Saint Philomena, Obatala and Saint Benedict, and Shango and Saint John.

Every orisha has a personality of its own, with preferred offerings and sacrifices, specific sacred numbers, and particular colors/garments that represent them. One can quickly identify the devotee to a particular orisha from his stylized behavior and clothing. For example, the orisha Shango is known to favor the colors red and white, and Ogun, the god of war, likes to receive roosters and rams as offerings. When it comes to spiritual possessions, each orisha has a piece of specific ritual music and dance associated with their summoning. A possessed medium will adopt the personality and accessories known to belong to the divine spirit. For example, a medium possessed by Ogun will be dressed in red and white, have a sword as a prop piece, and will behave in a violent, rough way. Most Creole religions have this theatrical side when it comes to communicating with their deities.

Every Shango shrine holds an annual celebration dedicated to the orisha that its believers worship. The ritual of celebration lasts for 4 days, and it starts off with prayers for the specific orisha, followed by several repetitions of Catholic prayers (Hail Mary, Lord's Prayer, and Apostle's Creed). The spiritual leader then recites a succession of prayers (such as Saint George's prayer, Blessed Mary's prayer, and so on depending on the preferred saints of the shrine) line-by-line, with the audience repeating each verse after him. After the prayers are done, a food offering is left outside for the trickster god Eshu to ensure that he won't meddle with the rituals. With Eshu pacified, the important part of the ritual finally provides. The drumming starts to invite the desired orisha to the celebration, usually starting off with Ogun's rhythm on the first night. The drumming, dancing, and singing continue to trigger the spiritual possession. At dawn, animal sacrifice is made to appease the orisha. The following three nights follow similar rituals, with the only difference being the summoned orisha and the animal sacrifice chosen.

The cult life of Shango worshippers from Trinidad closely resembles that of traditional African religions. They serve the orishas by having rituals dedicated to them. Providing them with food and animal offerings, holding divination sessions, and practicing conjuring ceremonies (which serve as a means of honoring the orisha). The devotees also serve the orishas by living their lives according to their teachings, advice, and prophecies.

The Santería Cult of Trinidad

Many elements of Santería are derived from Yoruba traditions and rituals. Some examples of adopted religious practices are ritual music. Traditional African drums and songs are used. People use the Yoruba dialect to sing, dancing with the dancers being possessed by the orishas, and animal sacrifices to appease and honor the spirits. The devotees wear religious items associated with the orishas (colored beads, specific garments), they cook and eat the meals that the orishas prefer. They use traditional Yoruba medicine to treat their ailments. Leaves and herbs with Yoruba names are also used to wash the stones of the orishas as well as the head of the cult members.

Just like the rest of the Creole religions, Santería associates orishas with Catholic saints. Orunmila, the prophet orisha, is identified with Saint Francis. Yemoja with the Virgin Mary of Regala. Shango is Saint Barbara, Eshu, the trickster, is Saint Peter, and the twin orishas Ibeji are assimilated with the saint Cosman and Damian.

For Santería ceremonies, the ritual objects (stones) and the priests are washed with special herbs to prepare them for contact with the orisha. The service starts with an animal sacrifice, and the stones of the high priest are soaked in the creature's blood. The Santería people believe that animal blood is the food of the orishas and that they need to be fed through the sacred stones. If the orisha is satisfied with the offering, a spiritual possession will occur. Ritual music is used to honor the orisha. Good Santería devotees make sure that their orishas are properly fed and satisfied to gain their favor and assistance in their daily lives.

The Vodou Cult and the Orishas

Vodou is a neo-African religion that combines the traditions and religious beliefs of the Yoruba, Lemba, Siniga, and Fon people with Roman Catholic practices and principles. The orishas of the Vodou cult are known as Iwa, and they have different origins, from African to Haitian and Christian. The orishas of the Vodou religion are spirits of nature and patrons of specific crafts. Popular nature deities are Bade, a spirit of wind; Dambala, a serpent spirit associated with the rainbow and the flooding season; and Agwé, a spirit of the sea. Additionally, there are two thunder deities, the Yoruba orisha Shango and the Fon spirit Sogbo.

The patron deities, also known as functional Iwa, include spirits from a wide array of cults. There is Legba, the spirits of crossroads and barriers (equivalent with the trickster god Eshu), who was associated with Saint Peter and Saint Anthony the Hermit. Ezili is a Fon goddess of the sea, considered to be the richest of the orishas, who is also worshiped as Mater

Dolorosa. The marassa (the twin spirits of death) are associated with saints Cosmas and Damian (equivalent with the Ibeji of Santería). Ogun Balanjo is a healer deity, linked with Saint Joseph, and Adja is a spirit of herbs and pharmacy.

Many of the deities are associated with Catholic saints or spirits from other cultures. There are many confusions and contradictions regarding the nature of the orishas. This is in part because Vodou mixes a wide variety of African-related belief systems but also because no written documents are detailing the hierarchy of the Vodou pantheon. Another element that deepens the confusion is the character of Vodou's spiritual possession. Devotees believe that during the possession trance, the medium acts and speaks in the name of the spirit. This means that the Vodou practitioners change their perception of a spirit based on how they behave in the course of the religious ceremony.

The Vodou devotees have a contractual-like relationship with their Iwa. If a person is diligent in their worship (provides the proper offerings and takes part in all the ceremonies), the spirits will be generous. The Vodou orishas are quite the needy ones, requiring frequent gifts and biannual payment. They enjoy animal sacrifices, and they are vengeful if ignored. It is known that an angered Iwa will cause misfortunes, such as bad luck, sickness, and even the death of family members.

In the Vodou belief, the spirits of the dead are also to be honored and catered to. That is why the practitioners of the religion pay a lot of attention to funeral rites (following Catholic traditions) and post-funeral rituals (the "last prayer" held on the ninth night after death, and the 10th-night sacrificial offering to appease the spirit). A dead family member must be mentioned in religious ceremonies, and annual memorial services are held to remember the departed spirit and avoid angering it. After the Iwa, the souls of the dead are the most respected spirits in Vodou religion.

The Shouters of Trinidad

Since we've started this presentation of religions with the most popular spiritual movement of Trinidad, it's fitting to end it on a similar note with the second-most practiced orisha cult of Trinidad, the Spiritual Baptist. Also known as Shouters, these religious practitioners don't use drums and rattles for their ritual music. They believe that only the Holy Spirit can possess the body of a devotee (but sometimes, Shango's spirit can take hold of someone during a particular ceremony). They bring offerings and make animal sacrifices to spirits of natural forces (orishas of the sea, the land, and so on). They have a special bond with Shango worshippers. Both Baptists and Shangoists are baptized by a Shouter pastor, and both cults celebrate the orisha of thunder, Shango.

It is not unusual for Shango devotees to attend Baptist ceremonial rites or for Shouters to take part in annual celebrations held by Shango shrines. Most Shouters have African descent, and they come from the lower class, the religion serving as a means of identifying themselves with their heritage.

Serving the Spirits

The various forms of orisha practice are prevalent in Trinidad and Tobago. People accept the practice because they resonate with the ideologies or because of family tradition, and it serves as a way for people to embrace their heritage and gain a sense of social identity. Although there are many distinctions between the Creole religions that worship orishas, we can establish a general explanation of what serving the orishas means to the people of Trinidad and Tobago.

Orishas are divine spirits that, if worshiped diligently, can bring forth good fortune, prosperity, and happiness. All orishas require frequent offerings of food and animal sacrifices, as well as annual celebrations and specific rituals. Those who dare ignore their orishas will face great misfortunes, as nothing is worse than an angered spirit. For the people of Trinidad and Tobago, serving the orishas is sort of like a full-time job. It comes with responsibilities and rules. Those that perform well get rewarded, while those that slack off will get punished.

However, the aspect of serving the divine spirits also works as a common ground for these various religious cults, allowing them to come together in times of need and celebrate their differences.

TEN

The Feast Season

The feast season, also known as Ebo, is a time of thanksgiving, unity, celebration, and sacrifice. An Ebo is filled with dance and music that go on from night till dawn, food, and spiritual manifestations of the celebrated orishas. It is a time when all African Caribbean people come together to celebrate their shared cultural experience and heritage but also their differences.

Since we have previously examined the topic of spiritual possession, you recognize by now the technicalities of the Ebo feast. There needs to be specific music and dancing to call upon the orisha. Then, the spirit takes over the medium and shares its wisdom. At the same time, the celebration continues with music, frenetic dancing, and food. The celebration ends at dawn with an animal sacrifice for the orisha in question. Then, everything is repeated the next night to honor a different orisha. That would be a summary of what happens during an Ebo. But, since this is a matter of utmost importance for the orisha devotees, we can't speak of a feast only in technical terms. The human element is crucial, and that is filled with emotions and raw sensations.

So, for this chapter, we'll get immersed into an orisha Ebo

feast by describing it from an outsider's view. It's a fun and simple way to vicariously experience a mesmerizing African-Caribbean ceremony.

The Orisha Shrine

One would probably assume that an orisha shrine would be tucked into the less-known corners of Trinidad, hidden from the prying eyes of the world. But, our Ebo takes place in central Trinidad, in a quaint and straightforward garden, where Shango, the god of thunder and lightning, will soon walk among its worshippers. The midnight sky is lightened ablaze by sparks of lightning, as to commemorate the special event. The shrine looks nothing like a Christian church.

It has a palais (an open part of the building) where the people have already gathered. Here the dancing, singing, and the spiritual manifestation will happen, an energetic celebration devoid of sinister aspects. In the four corners of the palais, candles are burning, their dancing flames enticing an eerie feeling of joy. In these candles, water or sweet essential oils will be poured as an offering to Shango. At the end of the palais, the three drummers have taken their place, ready to start signing the orisha's rhythm and move the souls of the audience. Facing the drummers, there is a sacred artifact, Ogun's sword, the weapon of the god of war, lodged into the ground - an African Excalibur. The blade is surrounded by candles, essential oils, water, and perhaps some rum to entice the orishas.

The chappelle is the room adjoined to the palais, housing items of worship. Here you can find statues of the orishas, images of them, Christian crucifixes, more candles, bottles of water and olive oil, and sacred items associated with the spirits. These items might seem common to the untrained eye. Nevertheless, they are sacred to the orisha devotees, as they represent the nature and personality of the spirits. Every chappelle has its collection of ceremonial brooms, shak-shaks (traditional African rattles), weapons (swords, cutlasses,

Shango's double-bladed wooden ax), shepherd's crooks, and thunderstones (stones taken from sacred places, through which an orisha can be "fed," these stones are usually placed on white plates and sprinkled with olive oil).

Outside, in the shrine's garden, there is the perogun, a place in which 20 bamboo trees have been planted to work as flag poles. Flags are considered to be channels that allow the spirits to visit the shrine, so they are crucial for the Ebo feast. The perogun also functions as a sacrificial spot for the poor animal that will be sacrificed to honor the orisha. Tonight, a red flag adorns the bamboo pole as an invitation to Shango.

Besides the perogun, the garden has many carefully planned installations. Stools and candles are scattered around to encourage the orishas. The water pond that, to the naked eye, looks like a decor piece, serves a higher purpose. Many orishas are water spirits. Their devotees believe that water acts as a pool of spiritual force, which would allow the orisha to possess the medium without tiring off their own spiritual power. Every piece of decor and installment of a shrine caters to the will and necessities of the orishas to make sure that the celebration will go smoothly. Most Orisha shrines have these same exact structures and spatial organization, with slight differences depending on which orishas are celebrated there.

The Ebo Feast

Inside the palais, the drums start their energetic rhythm, call-and-response ritual music, which involves the audience. The devotees start chanting and swaying their bodies, responding to the rhythm of the drums. Christian hymns and prayers turn into Yoruba songs as the music and the swaying induce a trance-like state. Musical offerings are made, all sung in the Yoruba language. The song leader sings for the orishas in a specific order, starting off with Eshu, the messenger deity, and continuing with whatever spirits the audience wants to honor. There is no liturgy or rules regarding the order of the songs. No one is scared of what is to come, and no one gets tired. Spiritual possession is a miraculous state in which the body feels no pain, and the main retains no memory. A medium that walks through fire or suffers some unfortunate accident while possessed will have no scars or symptoms the following day, nor will he remember the words of the orisha. Mediums put their whole trust into the spirits that take over them, and they let themselves be overrun with divine grace.

The ritual music continues, calling for Shango to manifest. It does not take long for an audience member to fall to the ground. The man's body shakes and turns uncontrollably, shaken by spasms. He awkwardly moves toward the palais, his feet barely remembering how to walk right and his face showing internal turmoil. Spiritual possession has a character of imprisonment to it, as the spiritual force of the orisha overtakes the body and throws aside the soul of the medium. This fight for control is accepted as something normal, and the medium will have no memory of the struggle once the orisha leaves him.

The path to the palais is sprinkled with olive oil, and a single candle waits on the doorstep. The man manages to get himself through the door frame, his massive body falling once again, in an abnormal position. The audience is not ecstatic, a sentiment fueled by the crescendo of the music, and the air is thick with incense (from oil offerings). Devotees gather around the man, ridding him of items that could hurt him (such as sharp jewelry), and his clothes are arranged to allow him to move freely. A red cloth piece is tied around his waist and shoulder, representing Shogun's specific attire.

The man is taken inside the shrine for more preparations, and when he emerges again, he can hardly be recognized. Gone is his awkward stance and his reserved demeanor. The man stands straight, brimming with confidence and authority. His hands are firmly clutched on the shepherd's crook as he surveys his flock. Shango watches his devotees with fatherly eyes as the drums keep their energetic rhythm. The sacred thunderstone is brought out and bathed with olive oil as Shango blesses each member of the ceremony.

But Shango did not come alone. To guard and protect the ceremony, his wife Oya has manifested herself in a white-robed woman from the audience. She is a violent spirit who walks around brandishing an ax to repel evil spirits and keep the audience in check. Oya moves around like a lioness in a cage, her ax glimmering in the candlelight. No one dares to defy her as she motions for them to enter the palais and kneel in front of her husband.

A Season of Celebration

The songs, dances, and blessings go on through the night. While the moon is still gracing the night sky, the drummers relocate to the perogun to welcome the people bringing sacrificial animals. The animal offerings are properly danced and sung, and finally, all is over. A designated cook prepares the meats for the orishas and audience to feast on, and the sacred thunderstorms are left to bathe in the sacrificial blood. Not all shrines practice animal sacrifices, though. Some offer fruits or spices that are known to be preferred by the orisha due to economic and moral reasons.

As the light of dawn bathes the devotees, the ceremony ends. The people are smiling, their faces radiant with spiritual enrichment. The nights to come will celebrate different orishas in similar patterns. After the feast season is done, the remaining food will be donated to the poor members of the district. Only the flags, fluttering away in the warm breeze, stand as proof of the nights of celebration.

There are more than 70 orisha shrines in Trinidad, and many of those celebrate Shango as the epitome of the Orisha faith. This religion is complex and hard to understand for outsiders. It is governed by esotericism and mysticism. It combines traditional African ideas and practices with Christianity, without weakening the African ideology of the cult. The worshippers use their practices and beliefs to express their cultural affinities, their heritage, and their acceptance of one another. Ebos are times of happiness and love, meant to honor the gods and bring communities together, even those of different faiths. It is not unheard of for Hindus and Spiritual Baptists (or other orisha-religions) to take part in the Ebos of other communities as a sign of solidarity and acceptance.

It is hard to capture the magic of the Caribbean feast in words. It's a cultural explosion of music, dance, and color that can never be fully comprehended by someone that did not grow up in the Orisha faith.

ELEVEN

Religion Today

According to a 2011 census, in Trinidad and Tobago, religious groups with African roots represent 6.6% of the entire population. However, this figure does not show the reality of the religious scene in the Caribbean country. This 6.6% comes from self-admitted Orisha followers and Spiritual Baptists. However, 11.1% of the population preferred to not specify their religious affinity, and 7.5% of the people who took part in the census-designated "other," which can consist of African cults.

While there is no means of identifying for sure how many people worship African deities, we do know that the ethnic and religious distribution of the islands is different. In Trinidad, only 32% of the population has African descent, out of which the majority are Christian, while in Tobago, 85% of the population has African roots, although they too are predominantly Christian. It is unclear how much these numbers are a true reflection of reality. Still, a rough estimate is that 10% of the population practices some sort of orisha worship.

The constitution of the Caribbean country allows people

to adhere to whatever religious cults they want and to practice their spiritual beliefs. And yet, society discriminates against African cults, and popular media still holds on to voodoo stereotypes. Voodoo is a term used to describe all Creole religions of Trinidad and Tobago, and it holds a negative connotation. Many Christian believers describe orisha worshippers as evil, demonic, and ill-intended, basing their judgment on myths and misconceptions. Nonetheless, the Orisha movement has been on the rise for the last couple of years. Its popularity is reaching new heights with the new generation's interest in connecting with their heritage and culture. As a result of its rise in popularity, the orisha religion has been officially recognized by cultural circles, society, politicians, and media outlets.

There are many reasons why the orisha religion is slowly but surely becoming a staple faith for the Creole people of Trinidad and Tobago. It managed to spread, adapt, and persist in times of hard discrimination. The orisha religion modified its beliefs to fit the social situation and struggles of the African and native people of Trinidad and Tobago. In this process, it gained a new meaning and purpose for its devotees. It promotes the value of family, the importance of nature, the connection to one's heritage and culture, and the acceptance of others. Through the orisha movement, the people get a sense of identity and a re-introduction to a piece of new ancient knowledge. The orisha priests are attractive figures who offer spiritual guidance, healing services, mental support, and emotional help. They help people solve their life problems and find their purpose, which makes them relatable and extremely approachable.

The religious world of Trinidad and Tobago is changing, and the law system is aware of that. Discrimination against one's religious beliefs is prohibited, as long as the religion does not promote hostility toward the government. Children are allowed to attend public schools regardless of their religious adherence. Expressions of hatred toward a person's spiritual beliefs are considered a felony. If someone displays indecent behavior in a place of worship or violently attacks someone's religion, they can get a massive fine of up to 1,000 TT (Trinidad and Tobago) dollars. Victims of religious discrimination can file for a judicial review of the person and have a chance of getting justice. The country of Trinidad and Tobago is making strides in truly accepting their religious diversity outside of touristic attractions and carnivals.

This does not indicate there is no more need for change. The orisha devotees still practice their rituals in secrecy. Their rituals and celebrations are not open to people outside their religious sphere unless they are considered trustworthy. They wear their colored beads, and they plant their flags, but their spiritual life remains as private as it ever was. No matter the ethical values they promote or the positive changes they make to their community. By helping one another and especially those in need, the Christian consensus remains the same. Orisha, a religion without a Devil, is a satanic belief that dabbles in witchcraft, spellcasting, and curses. All these are indeed part of an orisha-derived practice, that of Obeah. But, as I may have mentioned before in a previous chapter, the Obeah practice is almost extinct in our modern-day and age. The healers and mediums of the orisha religion are well-intended and kind. They seek to help their patients, and they use ancient recipes to cure physical and mental ailments. Long gone are the days of the fearful Obi-man and the old hag Obi-woman.

The reality is that people will always fear what they can't understand. And no joke, the orisha faith is one hard cookie to crack. The people have centuries of myths, traditions, and practices, most of which have been passed on exclusively through word of mouth. It's hard to grasp the mindset of an orisha follower if you were not born in an orisha-worshipping family. More so if you've never been part of one of their mesmerizing Ebo. All we can do is hope that society will continue to change for the better. That the Creole people of Trinidad and Tobago will be able to proudly express their religious beliefs without fear of discrimination of any kind.

TWELVE

Practices

Even though Trinidad is home to a wide array of Afro-Caribbean religions, they are similar enough for us to be able to speak of religious practices and traditions in general terms.

One important thing to know from the very beginning is that the Creole religions of Trinidad and Tobago don't have religious literature available for others to read and get initiated in their traditions and practices. Historically, information about these religious beliefs has been passed down orally, which leaves room for confusion and misinformation. However, nowadays, we have access to Afro-Caribbean literature written by scholars or practitioners, making Afro-Caribbean religions available to the vast population. It is thanks to books like African Religions: A Very Short Introduction by Jacob Olupona as well as other valuable pieces of literature that we can now get immersed into the exciting world of African religions.

General Caribbean Practices

Afro-Caribbean religions don't have a central religious authority (like the Catholics have the Pope, for example). They have initiates, priests, and high priests. Still, these figures are associated with a specific shrine, or at most, a city, not a leader accepted worldwide. But some orisha religions, including Lukumi and Santería, have a world spokesperson to represent the religious belief in official/mediatized scenarios. Apparently, the media loves to demonize the African-inspired religions, and it is a wise idea to have a trained individual deal with public meetings. Because of the negative way in which society regards them, Afro-Caribbean religions are veiled in secrecy. Rituals and ceremonies are meant only for priests, initiates, and loyal devotees, and the practices and traditions of each religion are kept behind closed doors as much as possible.

Now that we got that out of the way, let's talk about the practices of people from Trinidad and Tobago.

Worshiping Practices

As a part of their daily routines, devotees worship the orishas using altars in their homes, which can be dedicated to one or more divine spirits. This type of worship is called devotion. It consists of prayers, offerings (flowers, alcoholic beverages, fruits), and sometimes small animal sacrifices, such as hens, rabbits, or pigeons (depending on what the orisha prefers). The animal sacrifices usually need to be consecrated by a priest. These home altars are generally decorated with items associated with the specific orishas. For example, an altar for Yemoja will have blue and white pieces and a nautical theme, while an altar for Ogun will have weapons, wooden tools, and copper accessories.

Some religious practitioners feel the need to engage in rituals in the open air during the day. Quiet places are perfect for prayer sessions, and they offer the opportunity for a devotee to practice libation. The act of libation refers to pouring water outside or in a bowl/plant while naming deities or deceased family members (mainly in Vodou, where the spirits of the dead are feared). A libation is a form of honoring the spirits that can be easily included in the daily life routine of practitioners.

Most practitioners prefer to keep their rituals and prayers private, and it is unlikely for them to engage in devotion and worship outside of their homes and religious spaces. However, it is common for devotees to always have special items with them. These could be rocks, sticks, or other symbols of particular orishas. Or foods to get a sense of protection from the deities. These objects will most likely be kept hidden or in close proximity to the person just to ease their minds, and it is doubtful for them to be used for prayers.

Ceremonies and Rituals

A significant religious practice that's found in all Creole religions is divination. This ritual is done by a specialized priest, and its purpose is to gain guidance and advice from the orishas. It is an ancient oracle practice, similar to clairvoyance, that allows a devotee to contact a specific spirit and ask for help, with the help of an initiated medium. Divination is a private practice that shows the extent of the orishas' influence in the daily lives of their believers. Many religious practitioners believe that only through divination can one discover their purpose in the world and achieve their goal.

Religious services usually involve the use of ritual music (drumming and sacred songs) and dancing. Spiritual possession ceremonies utilize drumming and singing to call upon specific spirits to take over a medium and share their knowledge with the audience. It is common for the medium to be dressed in garments associated with the orisha and take upon the personality traits and mannerism of the spirit in question. Spiritual possession ceremonies are followed by an animal sacrifice to honor the orisha (or saint) and end with a communal feast to celebrate the occasion. Annual celebrations are commonly held to celebrate and recognize an orisha to gain his/her favor. Priests and priestesses are those who lead religious services, and most of these services are open and meant for big audiences.

Another essential religious practice of the people of

Trinidad and Tobago is ritual healing with the use of herbal medicine and guidance from the spirits. The healers are usually well-versed in the arts of root doctoring, and they have an exceptional understanding of how to use herbs and natural ingredients to cure ailments. Healers also take upon the role of spiritual advisers, mental health specialists, and emotional gurus to help a person defeat any obstacles they might be facing. In some religions, such as Vodou, a healer is also responsible for identifying diseases caused by hexes and ridding the person of the malevolent spell.

Diet and Clothing

When it comes to dietary restrictions, the orisha worshippers don't have strict rules, except fasting periods. Some devotees restrain themselves from drinking alcoholic beverages (especially priests) and eating fish or other meats (although vegetarianism is not imposed). Some foods that are associated with healing properties and living a healthy life are often adopted into the eating habits of religious practitioners. Because orisha devotees cherish their health, it is common for them to avoid fast-food, chemically altered products, additives, and canned food. They prefer to eat organic foods and cook their own meals, even for social events. Special food restrictions come from orisha worshippers who wish to respect the power source of their spiritual patron. For example, the orisha Oshun is said to hold her magic spells and her divine powers inside pumpkins, so as a sign of respect, her followers avoid eating the vegetable. However, offerings of pumpkin are made to Oshun to honor the deity.

There are no standardized religious attires made for daily wear, and most outfits are used for rituals and devotion purposes. The only instance when a religious garment is worn daily is when a person is going through initiation (to become priest/priestesses). They have to wear white long flowy clothes with white head coverings (scarves for women and hats for men) until their initiation period is over. But there are cult objects, such as amulets and beaded jewelry, worn daily by all devotees to gain spiritual protection and to identify a person as part of a particular religious category. The beads fit the color palette of the specific orisha who is worshipped (blue and white for Yemoja, red for Shango), and they are used for necklaces, bracelets, and ankle bracelets. The charms and amulets are also used to repel evil spirits and bring forth prosperity.

Traditions and Practices Linked to Life Events

Since religion is closely tied in with the significant events of a man's life, let's take a look at cultures and practices relating to birth, marriage, and death.

Birth

During childbirth, it is customary for mothers to have the support of older women from their families. The new mother is then expected to rest for almost two months, a period during which she and the newborn are being taken care of by female relatives and neighbors. That is in part because pregnant women and new mothers are vulnerable to health problems caused by supernatural powers (such as spells or hexes), and by staying inside, they minimize the risks. It is also common for the mother and the baby to wear charms and amulets to protect them from evil spirits.

Marriage

Weddings in Trinidad and Tobago are not arranged. It's up to the couple if they decide to tie the knot or not, although the approval of the parents (especially the mother) is desired. Traditional families were encouraged to have many children and to live close by to other family members so that they can help each other in times of need. Nowadays, young Caribbean people marry at a later age and prefer a small family and more independence from their parents and relatives.

Marriage customs are mostly influenced by culture, and few African-religions have wedding-related rituals. Santería practitioners, for example, have a Catholic wedding ceremony followed by Santería ceremonies consisting of rituals, prayers, and food offerings to honor the orishas. Vodou practitioners have an interesting wedding ceremony in which one can marry a spirit. This ritual is similar to the spiritual possession one. Still, in this case, the ritual music and dancing are used to convince the spirit to marry the individual. Some standard wedding practices include invitations done through word-of-mouth and black wedding cakes (a special cake made with dried fruits and soaked in rum).

Legal marriages among orisha practitioners are not that common. Most couples chose to live together without being married. On the other hand, many continue to live with their parents while being in a relationship. The head of the family is typically the woman, and the maternal grandmother is seen as an extremely important family member who will have a significant role in raising and educating the children.

Divorce is not seen as a sin or an insult toward the orishas. People can move on and restart their lives with different partners without facing the wrath of their divine spirits.

Death and Funeral Traditions

Extended family is seen as very important in the Afro-Caribbean faith, and a person on their deathbed is very likely to receive many visitors. It is expected of people to take time off work and visit their ailing relative, no matter how distant it may be. Funerals are seldomly done after a person has died. It is usually delayed for as long as two weeks to ensure that all family members (especially those from other countries) can attend. A wake lasting about three days is held before the funeral to commemorate the deceased person.

There are many rituals and ceremonies associated with funerals, but not much is known or understood about them. The Vodou people believe that humans have a guardian soul (gwo bonanj) and a spirit (Iwa) and that the guardian soul needs to be removed from the body through a special ritual.

This death ritual allows for the spirit to communicate with family members in spiritual possession ceremonies.

The dead are usually hugely respected by the followers of African-Caribbean religions. They will honor them in special ceremonies, mention their names during rituals, and ask for their advice (through divination or spiritual possessions) whenever they feel lost.

THIRTEEN

Celebrations

Because the orisha religions of Trinidad and Tobago are deeply embedded into the culture and the social lives of their followers, it would be a shame to not get to know the people a little bit better. And what more excellent way to understand more about a group of people than by observing what they celebrate? Festivals, carnivals, and celebration days are often times when the culture and traditions of a population shine through the most.

Keep in mind that I'll only focus on celebrations that are relevant to our demographic, which means that this chapter won't present all the essential festivals of Trinidad and Tobago. There are plenty of Christian, Hindu, and Islamic celebrations that I'll skip, as well as music and food festivals that have little to no spiritual or cultural importance for the Creole population of the Caribbean islands. Ethnic diversity makes Trinidad and Tobago a country with many reasons to celebrate. I warmly recommend checking out the whole variety of festivals that it has to offer.

Spiritual Baptist Day

Also known as the Shouters Liberation Day, this celebration takes place on March 30th. It commemorates the abolition of the Shouter Prohibition Ordinance, which banned Spiritual Baptists from practicing their religion.

This ordinance was approved in 1917, simply because the colonial law perceived the Shouters' loud singing and dancing as a threat (although it was clearly just an annoyance). The truth behind this religious ban has nothing to do with the disturbance of public peace or with the law feeling threatened. In that period of time, even though slavery was abolished, the white population (which represented the minority) was not thrilled about the resilience of the African culture and traditions. They were especially displeased with the Spiritual Baptist Church, as it blended Christian beliefs and concepts with African customs and ideas. The colonials in power did not agree with the public, communal displays of African traditions, and the decree was created in an attempt to stifle the practice of African-inspired religions.

The roots of the Shouter religion were as diverse as the ethnic groups that lived together on the islands. Spiritual Baptism was initially brought to Trinidad and Tobago by Merikins. These were the African-American free slaves and refugees of the British-American war of 1812. Because they fought for the British, they were settled in the south of Trinidad, in company villages. Their Baptist faith drew inspirations from the evangelical sects of southern slave states and from traditional African forms of worship. So, when the British Baptists visited Trinidad, they were shocked by the "primitive" forms of worship that the Shouters had. The most alarming feature of the Spiritual Baptist services was the shouting used as a way of expressing one's belief and devotion. That is why the Spiritual Baptists were dubbed "Shouters," a mean moniker meant to show the disgust of the Christian Baptists.

Even if the shouting was the "trademark" of their religious services, the Spiritual Baptist had many other fascinating facets of their religious practices. They had spiritual possession ceremonies in which the Holy Spirit took hold of the devotees, which led to frenetic dancing, singing, and speaking in native African dialects. They also had usual Baptist rituals, blended with traditional touches such as the mournin process. The mournin is a practice in which the devotees have their eyes covered. They are left to sit or kneel on the bare ground for up to a week, without access to food or water. Through mournin, the person experiences a symbolic death and resurrection, and their sins are forgiven. In other words, the person gets a new beginning in life, a chance to become a better version of themselves. Spiritual Baptism services included the use of chanting, symbolic colors, special garments, and accessories. There are bells, flags, and drums, making it more similar to Vodou and Santería than Christian Baptism. This diversity of African influences made the Christian population assume the worst, with fears of black magic and Obeah practice fueling the public opinion.

The ordinance was officially repealed in 1951, meaning that for 34 years, the Shouters were forced to practice their religious beliefs in secrecy, with the constant fear of being discovered and punished by the law. Many people were arrested and fined for expressing their religious beliefs. It was only due to the rise of the anti-colonial sentiment that spiritual freedom was granted.

As the people struggled for religious freedom even after the repeal, in 1996, the holiday was publicly recognized. It was a governmental attempt to patch up the mistakes of the past. Today, the Spiritual Baptist religion is thriving, and March 30th is an important day of celebration.

Tobago Heritage Festival

The Tobago Heritage festival lasts for two weeks and runs from mid-July to the beginning of August. It is a major annual event that celebrates the unique culture of Tobago, from its bélè dances to its traditional foods and exotic music. The festival is a time of revival for the cultural essence of Tobago, and it is treasured by both locals and tourists.

The Heritage Festival was first held in 1987. Since then, it has risen to fame, becoming the main event of celebration for the Tobago people. The artistic programs take place in small and picturesque villages, giving more authenticity to the productions. This festival allows tourists to discover the island and its traditions by hopping from one community to another. Most events are held at night, the magical atmosphere enchanting visitors and immersing them into the mesmerizing yet straightforward lives of the Tobago people.

The festival starts with a gala, and during the two-week schedule, many exciting events take place. The Ole Time Tobago Wedding (also known as Ole Time Wedding in Moriah) is a public re-enactment of an 18th-century bridal procession. The people walk around the streets of the Moriah village dressed in period-accurate attire, charming the audiences. Other re-enactment events include a post-emancipation labor riot from 1876 known as the Belmana Riots. Also, the Salaka Feast. Traditional celebrations resemble the Ebo feasts, started by the plantation workers who came to Tobago post-emancipation to help its shambling economy.

There are also fun events, such as the Goat Races and the Bucco Crab Races, which energize the audiences. The Goat Race is similar to a horse racing competition, in the sense that a jockey and a goat team up to defy all odds and cross the finish line.

The Crab Race is a bit different. In this event, each participant picks a crab, which gets marked with a little name tag. Next, the crabs are put in a bucket placed upside down in the middle of a set of concentric circles. When the race time is on, the bucket is raised. The winner is the first crab to make it to the outside of the circles. These races provide entertainment and engage the audiences, which are encouraged to place bets on their favorites to raise the stakes.

There is still the Miss Heritage Personality Contest, a popularity contest in which women are graded based on their contribution to their communities rather than by their appearances.

The Tobago Heritage Festival allows visitors to explore the aspects of the island's past. It is a pure expression of the soul and cultural essence of the Tobago people.

The Carnival

The Carnival of Trinidad and Tobago is a two-day extravagant celebration that matches the likes of the Rio and New Orleans carnivals.

Although it is not recognized as an official holiday, every citizen of Trinidad and Tobago takes their time to publicly celebrate the occasion by dancing in the streets, jumping around, and engaging in the general excitement and fun of the Carnival.

The Carnival does not have a strict schedule like the Tobago Heritage Festival. It usually starts right after the Christmas celebrations are done, and the season of the flesh begins. The term Carnival is loosely translated from Latin to "farewell to the flesh," and the celebration comes from religious roots. After the holy observation of Christmas, the people were allowed to party and enjoy themselves one last time before entering the Lenten season, a period of fasting and piety.

During those days of fun, the people of the lower social classes (the upper classes only watched for afar) would be in a generalized state of frenzy, dancing, singing, and creating colorful characters who are still portrayed in the modern Carnival celebrations.

Popular Carnival characters are Jab Jab, an impish horned creature that brandishes a three-pronged fork. Dame Lorraine, a beautiful woman with an ample bosom. Also, the Midnight Robber (a character that wears a wide-brimmed hat and speaks in "robber talk"; rhymes are used to tell stories of the robber's deeds). A popular event of the Carnival is the Steelpan festival, in which musicians show their mastery of the steel drums in an artistic competition.

The modern Carnival starts with an Opening Day, followed by the two days of intense partying. The rhythm of the Carnival is composed of a wide variety of tunes, from traditional calypso songs to soca beats, pop tunes, reggae vibes, and various popular hits. The Carnival is full of music, drama, street parades, and art. Each Carnival camp has its own traditions, culture, and ways of making mass (the creation of costumes or art pieces made to be worn). The costumes are ways in which each group expresses its heritage. Some use glitter and beads, while others go for sequins and feathers, and the more adventurous ones opt for body paint.

The Trinidad and Tobago Carnival is a once in a lifetime experience that never fails to attract tourists.

The Emancipation Day

On August 1st, the people of Trinidad and Tobago celebrate the end of slavery, when the Africans of the Caribbean were finally freed. Emancipation Day is recognized as a public holiday, and the celebration consists of street processions, cultural performances, religious observances, and a whole variety of other events.

Although the British parliament abolished the slave trade in 1807, it took several more decades for the existing slaves to escape the shackles of their masters. The emancipation movement gained traction due to the changes brought by the Industrial Revolution and to the rise in popularity of the humanitarian groups. On August 1st, 1834, the Emancipation bill came into effect, bringing about the freedom of 20,000 Trinidad and Tobago slaves. Over 150 years later, the government of Trinidad and Tobago declared Emancipation Day a national holiday. It became the first country to have a national holiday that celebrates the abolition of the slave trade and slavery.

In Trinidad and Tobago, the week before the Emancipation Day is marked by cultural activities, such as music performances, dances, and traditional songs. Artists from all around the globe gather to the dual-island country to celebrate the African people of the Caribbean world. Art exhibitions and public lectures held by African scholars are also part of the preparation for the events of the Emancipation Day.

The street procession that takes place on the first day of celebration is known as The Kamboule. It is basically a theater in motion that walks the streets of the capital city Port of Spain. Here, one can see the famous Moko Jumbie, traditional dance groups, African drums, and steelpan performers putting on a show for the public. The people dress in their best traditional African garments, and they clap, chant, and dance to commemorate their past and wish for a brighter future. The atmosphere is similar to that of a carnival, but it has subtle grave undertones.

The day ends on a strong note, with a re-enactment of the African rebellion against plantation owners and slave masters (known as the Flambeau Procession). During this time of celebration, visitors have the chance to experience an important event in African culture. Lucky tourists can go home with authentic African artifacts, such as paintings, amulets, and garments that are sold in the marketplace (helping the local economy).

FOURTEEN

Ritual Music

Music is an enormous part of the Orisha religion. Traditional songs, dances, and drumming are essential to orisha worshipping and celebration. Ritual music is often the only common ground of the numerous sects that practice African-inspired traditions.

Ritual Music in Trinidad

In Trinidad, music is used in ebos (feasts) and religious ceremonies that host spiritual possessions. In such ceremonies, the call and response ritual music is performed. The musician uses a triad of drums called the conga, the bemba, and the oumalay (derived from the Yoruba bata drum) to sing polyrhythmic tunes. The audience uses traditional instruments, including the shak-shak (a type of rattle), to respond to the rhythm of the drums. It is also common for the devotees to respond to the drums by clapping their hands or by merely dancing to the rhythm. The use of the drums is carefully choreographed as each orisha requires a very specific amalgamation of drumming and signing. These particular patterns are considered sacred, and they are preserved and passed down from generation to generation.

Although each ceremony and celebration requires

different music, the three drums have their particularities that set them apart. The bemba is always the lead, and it delivers a syncopated rhythm when slapped. The congo followed the lead of the bemba and comes in with its fast repetitive patterns. And last but not least, the oumalay is the improviser of the group. The drum takes on the role of creating complex polyrhythms against the combined patterns of the bemba and the congo. This trio of drums is used to express adoration for the orisha, to devote animal sacrifices and offerings to the deities, and to call on a particular orisha for spiritual possessions.

Typical celebrations start with Christian prayers, mainly Hail Marys, accompanied by soft drumming. Then, all music stops for a brief time before starting back again, this time with the drums taking the lead and the music shifting to traditional African songs. Invitation music is sung in the Yoruba dialect. Asking for the orisha to visit the ceremonies and possess the devotees. Acceptance songs show the people's gratitude after the manifestation of a divine spirit, and work songs are uttered when the orisha is offering advice and guidance through a medium.

Music in Trinidad serves two purposes. There is a religious one and a social one. Orisha worshippers are mainly people of the working-class. This traditional music serves as a force of solidarity of the community, and it encompasses the identity of the Orisha devotees. The people of Trinidad take a lot of pride in their music, as it has the power to bring them together.

The creole sects of Trinidad use African traditions with cultural influences from French religious practices. An example of this is the bélè, a courtship dance created by African slaves as an imitation of French ballroom dances. It combines moves from traditional African fertility dances with French contredanse. A dance for several couples, in which every couple dances its way to the head of a double line formed by all-men and all-women sides. The bélè starts off elegantly as the original French dance. Still, the rhythm of the drums changes along the way to an energetic tune. As the rhythm accelerates, the dancers gather around the drummers, and their moves become more dynamic and sensual. The rhythm is polyphonic, swaying from slow to fast as the dance continues. Just like the traditional Orisha musicians, the creole singers use three drums that have similar roles as the bemba, congo, and oumalay.

The Spiritual Baptists from Trinidad, also known as Shouters, are famous for their syncretic music practices. Their music tradition comes from North American styles, Anglican hymns, and African call and response music. However, since their settling in Trinidad, the Spiritual Baptists have adopted a new array of ritual music, such as Yoruba rhythms, Chinese vocalization, Hindu devotional music, and African-American spiritualism. This function of different elements is known as doption singing. It calls for a spiritual experience consisting of the Holy Spirit taking the devotee on a mental journey, a Christian form of spiritual possession. Doption music usually starts off with harmonized Anglican hymns accompanied by traditional African drumming (with clapping and shouts from the audience) and followed by vocalizations and melodies from different cultures. The audience always participates by swaying or dancing and singing in various dialects in response to the music.

Ritual Music in Tobago

The Tobago reel is a piece of syncretic ritual music derived from traditional Scottish music because Scottish planters inhabited the small island in the colonial era. The reel is basically an Africanized Scottish dance and song used both for celebration purposes and religious ceremonies (mainly spiritual possessions). The reel features typical instruments (fiddles, tambourines, and idiophone, or triangle) and a singer. The music fits the Scottish folk genre, and it combines the Scottish tradition of combining tunes to create continuous melodies with the African approach of interweaving drum patterns to create constant rhythms.

The Tobago reel is known to last from 6 pm until 6 am the following morning in devotional ceremonies. It is known to produce a trance-like state that allows the spirits to be called upon for prophecies and advice.

FIFTEEN

The Evolution of the Orisha Religious System

The Orisha religion of Trinidad and Tobago has its origins in the colonial era. When the constant oppression endured by the African people made them rely on their old deities, more than ever before. Religion became a sort of system of resistance for them, a representation of the will of the Creole people and their resilience to never give up on their spiritual identity. The Orisha religion became a means of cultural consolidation for the African people because it connected them on a deep spiritual level, a profound bond that went beyond the color of the skin. The Christian churches attempted time and time again to demonize and criminalize the orisha practices but to no avail.

The Orisha religion prevailed in Trinidad and Tobago due to several factors. For one, the number of people of African descent who came to the dual-insular country greatly exceeded that of Caucasian colonials and plantation owners. Even today, people with African ancestry are a majority in Trinidad and Tobago.

Second, the West African people arrived in the Caribbean world relatively late. Meaning their religious beliefs were already fully formed and rock-solid in their minds and souls.

And last but not least, the Orisha religion prevailed because its structure of beliefs and its system is flexible and extremely adaptable. It allows for new elements to be added in and incorporated into religious practice without diminishing its importance or compromising its authenticity.

The term orisha is made of two words, ori, which in Yoruba means "head," and se, which translates to "source." So orishas, the deities, come from the ultimate source of everything, Olorun, the supreme creator. In the Orisha religion, everything links back to Olorun and their spiritual energy. By the end of the 19th century, the Orisha religious system was made out of a mish-mash of beliefs and practices that have their roots in Yoruba cults.

The devotees adopted Christian customs and used them to hide their own traditions and beliefs. Integrating elements that suited their visions of the orishas and managing to combine theologies that seemed, at best, contradictory. Their places of worship or shrines are dedicated to any number of deities. All of which are celebrated and honored during the Ebo season. This allows for all the ancient orishas to be remembered and worshipped, as well as for new orishas to be recognized and integrated. The majority of shrines are private properties owned by women who are in charge of the places of worship. Women are highly respected and esteemed in African communities. Being considered more reliable than men (although there are still ritual functions that are administered exclusively by men).

The Orisha faith has triggered social growth and progress in the recent history of Trinidad and Tobago. The Black Power movement of the 1970s, for example, was one of great importance for the devotees of the orisha religion. Many young people of African ancestry returned to their ancestral practices and traditions as a way to ease their social and political frustrations and as a means of satisfying their spiritual needs. Through the Orisha religion, these young African people rebelled against the colonial arrangements that they inherited from their ancestors. Then, in 1988, the spiritual leader of the Orisha community, Ooni of Ife, visited Trinidad and Tobago. Ooni of Ife putting in place a local religious system for the orisha community, giving another boost to the spiritual movement. Finally, in 1997, the switch to a Hindu political power definitively shattered the Christian hegemony that was accepted in post-colonial Trinidad and Tobago. This lead to the official recognition of the Orisha faith and the legalization of Orisha practices. African religions were finally accepted and encouraged by Caribbean law.

With official recognition came more changes to the orisha religious system. More people openly declared affiliation with the orisha faith, including artists and middle to high-class members. The deities are starting to be worshipped under their real names and identities, no longer hiding under their Christian masks. The entire personality of the religion turned back to its African roots, and the practices are more and more creolized. Trinidad and Tobago is undergoing a time of religious revival, with the African people taking back their culture and proudly showing it to the world.

Conclusion

The Orisha religion of Trinidad and Tobago has had its ups and downs. It went from being practiced under the veil of Christianity to an expression of African identity, and finally, being recognized as an official religion protected by the law.

There are many facets to the orisha religions of the world. They have humanized deities, who are prone to making mistakes and who sometimes fall victim to their own vanity. Each orisha has its own personality that changes along with the orisha belief system to better fit the needs of the Creole people. Orishas are deities who seek to connect with their worshippers and guide them throughout their lives if the followers have honored them properly. Spiritual possessions are sacred ceremonies that allow the spirits to manifest among their devotees and share their knowledge. Ebo feasts are celebrations meant to honor the orishas and to bring communities together in a time of joy and spiritual enrichment.

Many practices and traditions of the Orisha people are based around serving their deities in the hope of gaining their favor and living a good, prosperous life. Some religious practices are private, like praying and making offerings on home altars, while others are communal events of worshiping.

Healing is seen as an essential part of the orisha way, which combines traditional roo-doctoring with the benevolence and aid of the orishas. Music and dance also hold a special place in the orisha tradition, allowing the people to express their culture and connect with their spiritual guides.

As with many other religions, there are good and bad parts. For every healer, there's an Obeah practitioner, a master of dark arts who specializes in hexes and spells. But the Obi-men of the present are much more docile and focused on doing good than the fearsome spellcasters of the colonial era. Orisha practitioners are slowly adapting to modern times, and their tightly knit communities become even tighter.

This book only presented the known facts of the Orisha religion. Many rituals, ceremonies, and practices are kept secret from the outside world to protect the faith system and its devotees. We may never truly understand the Orisha way of life, but I hope that now you know a little bit more than you did before.

References

Advameg Inc. (n.d.). Olorun - Myth Encyclopedia - mythology, god, legend, creation, life, king, people, African. Retrieved March 5, 2020, from www.mythencyclopedia.com website: http://www.mythencyclopedia.com/Ni-Pa/Olorun.html

African American Registry. (2018, November 12). Shango, an African based religion. Retrieved March 5, 2020, from African American Registry website: https://aaregistry.org/story/shango-an-african-based-religion/

Anderson/Sankofa, D. A. (1991). Creation Stories. Retrieved March 5, 2020, from Uga.edu website: http://www.gly.uga.edu/railsback/CS/CSGoldenChain.html

Bazinet, R. J. (2015). The Sonic Structure of Shango Feasts. Retrieved March 5, 2020, from Ethnomusicology Review website: https://ethnomusicologyreview.ucla.edu/journal/volume/20/piece/877

Boodan, S. (2019, July 27). Take a look at the Salaka Feast. Retrieved March 5, 2020, from www.guardian.co.tt website: https://www.guardian.co.tt/article/take-a-look-at-the-salaka-feast-6.2.895098.369055cff5

Brereton, B. M., Robinson, A. N. R., & Watts, D. (2019). Trinidad and Tobago - History. In *Encyclopædia Britannica*.

Retrieved from https://www.britannica.com/place/Trinidad-and-Tobago/History

Canson, P. E., & McKenna, A. (2014). Yemonja | Yoruban deity | Britannica. In *Encyclopædia Britannica*. Retrieved from https://www.britannica.com/topic/Yemonja

Caribmondo. (n.d.). Trinidad and Tobago. Shango, sticking to roots. – CARIBMONDO. Retrieved March 5, 2020, from caribmondo.com website: https://caribmondo.com/2020/01/05/trinidad-and-tobago-shango-sticking-to-roots/

Commonwealth Secretariat. (2017). Trinidad and Tobago: History | The Commonwealth. Retrieved March 5, 2020, from Thecommonwealth.org website: https://thecommonwealth.org/our-member-countries/trinidad-and-tobago/history

CubanYoruba. (2014). YORUBA RELIGION: SHANGO. Retrieved March 5, 2020, from YORUBA RELIGION website: https://cubanyoruba.blogspot.com/2007/05/shango.html

Davis, N. (2013, August 13). Resurgence of Jamaican "Voodoo." *BBC News*. Retrieved from https://www.bbc.com/news/world-latin-america-23166213

De-Light, D. (2001, January 2). Making mas. Retrieved March 5, 2020, from Caribbean Beat Magazine website: https://www.caribbean-beat.com/issue-47/making-mas#axzz6Fj3Ogh2a

Destination Trinidad and Tobago. (n.d.-a). 20 Festivals You Must Experience in Trinidad & Tobago: Destination Trinidad and Tobago | Tours, Holidays, Vacations and Travel Guide. Retrieved March 5, 2020, from destinationtnt.com website: https://www.destinationtnt.com/blog/a-land-of-endless-festivals/

Destination Trinidad and Tobago. (n.d.-b). Tobago Heritage Festival: Destination Trinidad and Tobago | Tours, Holidays, Vacations and Travel Guide. Retrieved March 5,

2020, from destinationtnt.com website: https://www.destinationtnt.com/events/tobago-heritage-festival/

Discover Trinidad & Tobago. (2018, March 27). Spiritual (Shouter) Baptist Liberation Day. Retrieved March 5, 2020, from Discover Trinidad & Tobago website: https://www.discovertnt.com/spiritual-shouter-baptist-liberation-day#axzz6EgJLagpO

Discover Trinidad & Tobago. (2018, July 25). Emancipation Day. Retrieved March 5, 2020, from Discover Trinidad & Tobago website: https://www.discovertnt.com/emancipation-day/#axzz6Fi1RuEKY

Encyclopedia of African-American Culture and History. (2020a, January 21). Healing, and the Arts in Afro-Caribbean Cultures | Encyclopedia.com. Retrieved March 5, 2020, from www.encyclopedia.com website: https://www.encyclopedia.com/history/encyclopedias-almanacs-transcripts-and-maps/healing-and-arts-afro-caribbean-cultures

Encyclopedia of African-American Culture and History. (2020b, January 29). Divination and Spirit Possession in the Americas | Encyclopedia.com. Retrieved March 5, 2020, from www.encyclopedia.com website: https://www.encyclopedia.com/history/encyclopedias-almanacs-transcripts-and-maps/divination-and-spirit-possession-americas

Encyclopedia of African-American Culture and History. (2020c, March 3). Orisha. Retrieved March 5, 2020, from www.encyclopedia.com website: https://www.encyclopedia.com/history/encyclopedias-almanacs-transcripts-and-maps/orisha

Encyclopedia of Religion. (2020a, January 25). Caribbean Religions: Afro-Caribbean Religions | Encyclopedia.com. Retrieved March 5, 2020, from www.encyclopedia.com website: https://www.encyclopedia.com/environment/encyclopedias-almanacs-transcripts-and-maps/caribbean-religions-afro-caribbean-religions

Encyclopedia of Religion. (2020b, February 11). Afterlife: African Concepts | Encyclopedia.com. Retrieved March 5, 2020, from www.encyclopedia.com website: https://www.encyclopedia.com/environment/encyclopedias-almanacs-transcripts-and-maps/afterlife-african-concepts

Encyclopedia of World Mythology. (2020, February 10). Olorun | Encyclopedia.com. Retrieved March 5, 2020, from Encyclopedia.com website: https://www.encyclopedia.com/history/encyclopedias-almanacs-transcripts-and-maps/olorun

Forde, M. (2019). The Spiritual Baptist Religion. *Caribbean Quarterly*, *65*(2), 212. Retrieved from https://www.academia.edu/39211185/The_Spiritual_Baptist_Religion

Funk, R. (2018, February 1). Walk tall, moko jumbie | Closeup. Retrieved March 5, 2020, from Caribbean Beat Magazine website: https://www.caribbean-beat.com/issue-149/walk-tall-closeup#axzz6FXImCUS0

GlobalSecurity.org. (n.d.). Trinidad & Tobago - Religion. Retrieved March 5, 2020, from www.globalsecurity.org website: https://www.globalsecurity.org/military/world/caribbean/tt-religion.htm

GoToStCroix.com. (2010, October 18). St. Croix Blog, The Mocko Jumbie: A Cultural Icons | GoToStCroix.com. Retrieved March 5, 2020, from | GoToStCroix.com website: https://www.gotostcroix.com/st-croix-blog/the-moko-jumbie-a-cultural-icon/

Government of the Republic of Trinidad and Tobago. (2020a). Emancipation Day. Retrieved March 5, 2020, from Ttconnect.gov.tt website: http://www.ttconnect.gov.tt/gortt/portal/ttconnect/

Government of the Republic of Trinidad and Tobago. (2020b). Tobago Heritage Festival. Retrieved March 5, 2020, from Ttconnect.gov.tt website: http://www.ttconnect.gov.tt/gortt/portal/ttconnect/

Government of the Republic of Trinidad and Tobago. (2020c). Trinidad and Tobago Carnival. Retrieved March 5,

2020, from Ttconnect.gov.tt website: http://www.ttconnect. gov.tt/gortt/portal/ttconnect/

Haines, L. (1972, September 10). Obeah Is a Fact of Life, and Afterlife, in the Caribbean. *The New York Times*. Retrieved from https://www.nytimes.com/1972/09/10/archives/ obeah-is-a-fact-of-life-and-afterlife-in-the-caribbean-obeah-a-fact.html

Henry, F. (2003). *Reclaiming African religions in Trinidad: the socio-political legitimation of the Orisha and spiritual Baptist faiths.* Barbados: University Of The West Indies Press; London. (Original work published 2020)

IIWINC. (2004a). Creole Religions in the Caribbean | Caribya! Retrieved March 5, 2020, from caribya.com website: http://caribya.com/caribbean/religion/creole/

IIWINC. (2004b). The Caribbean Religion | Caribya! Retrieved March 5, 2020, from Caribya.com website: http:// caribya.com/caribbean/religion/

IndexMundi. (2019, December 7). Trinidad and Tobago Religions - Demographics. Retrieved March 5, 2020, from www.indexmundi.com website: https://www.indexmundi. com/trinidad_and_tobago/religions.html

Laycock, J. (2015). *Spirit possession around the world: possession, communion, and demon expulsion across cultures.* Santa Barbara, California: Abc-Clio. (Original work published 2020)

Lonely Planet. (2017). History in Trinidad & Tobago. Retrieved March 5, 2020, from Lonely Planet website: https://www.lonelyplanet.com/trinidad-tobago/background/ history/a/nar/f9f3d6d1-851a-49ba-90c1-2386f23a98bb/358182

Maureen Warner Lewis. (1997). *Trinidad Yoruba: from mother tongue to memory/ Maureen Warner-Lewis.* Tuscaloosa: University Of Alabama Press. (Original work published 2020)

Moodley PhD, R., Sutherland, P., & Chevannes, B. (2013, July). Spirit-based healing in the Black diaspora. Retrieved March 5, 2020, from www.bacp.co.uk website: https://www.

bacp.co.uk/bacp-journals/therapy-today/2013/july-2013/spirit-based-healing-in-the-black-diaspora/

Nissen, J. (2018, June 2). Trinidad & Tobago: A Rich History of Dance, Devotion and Demonstration - Guide to the World of Music. Retrieved March 5, 2020, from Guide to the World of Music website: https://www.guidetotheworldofmusic.com/people-and-places/trinidad-tobago-a-rich-history-of-dance-devotion-and-demonstration/

Office Holidays. (n.d.). Spritual Baptist Day in Trinidad and Tobago in 2020. Retrieved March 5, 2020, from Office Holidays website: https://www.officeholidays.com/holidays/trinidad-and-tobago/spritual-baptist-day

Ogden, J. (2015, October 13). Family Fun at the Crab Races. Retrieved March 5, 2020, from | GoToStCroix.com website: https://www.gotostcroix.com/st-croix-blog/family-fun-crab-races/

Richards, P. (1999, August 19). RELIGION-TRINIDAD AND TOBAGO: Orisha Practice on the Move | Inter Press Service. Retrieved March 5, 2020, from www.ipsnews.net website: http://www.ipsnews.net/1999/08/religion-trinidad-and-tobago-orisha-practice-on-the-move/

Rinalducci, N. (2013). Issue 2 The Challenges of Teaching Sociology Article 3 Religious Pluralism: Sociology and Faith in a Caribbean Island. *The Journal of Public and Professional Sociology The Journal of Public and Professional Sociology*, *5*(2). Retrieved from https://digitalcommons.kennesaw.edu/cgi/viewcontent.cgi?referer=https://www.google.com/&httpsredir=1&article=1042&context=jpps

Saunders, C., & Allen, P. J. (2019, May 19). OLORUN - the Yoruba Supreme God (Yoruba mythology). Retrieved March 5, 2020, from Godchecker - Your Guide to the Gods website: https://www.godchecker.com/yoruba-mythology/OLORUN/

Scranton, L., & Stefon, M. (2016). Shango | Yoruba deity

| Britannica. In *Encyclopædia Britannica*. Retrieved from https://www.britannica.com/topic/Shango

Sen Nag, O. (2018, June 19). Religious Beliefs In Trinidad And Tobago. Retrieved March 5, 2020, from WorldAtlas website: https://www.worldatlas.com/articles/religious-beliefs-in-trinidad-and-tobago.html

Smithsonian Magazine. (2007, November 6). Trinidad and Tobago - History and Heritage. Retrieved March 5, 2020, from Smithsonian Magazine website: https://www.smithsonianmag.com/travel/trinidad-and-tobago-history-and-heritage-17893991/

Solimar Otero, & Toyin Falola. (2013). *Yemoja: gender, sexuality, and creativity in the Latina/o and Afro-Atlantic diasporas.* Albany: Suny Press. (Original work published 2020)

SouthWorld. (2016, October). Trinidad and Tobago. Shango, sticking to roots. Retrieved March 5, 2020, from www.southworld.net website: https://www.southworld.net/trinidad-and-tobago-shango-sticking-to-roots/

Sutherland, P., Moodley, R., & Chevannes, B. (2014). *Caribbean healing traditions: implications for health and mental health.* New York: Routledge. (Original work published 2020)

TANENBAUM. (n.d.). Afro-Caribbean | Tanenbaum.org. Retrieved March 5, 2020, from tanenbaum.org website: https://tanenbaum.org/religion-at-work-resource/religions-of-the-world/afro-caribbean/

The Editors of Encyclopaedia Britannica. (2018, February 23). African religions. Retrieved March 5, 2020, from Encyclopedia Britannica website: https://www.britannica.com/topic/African-religions#ref810938

The Wanderling. (n.d.-a). OBEAH: Afro-Caribbean Shamanism. Retrieved March 5, 2020, from www.angelfire.com website: http://www.angelfire.com/electronic/awakening101/obeah.html

The Wanderling. (n.d.-b). OBEAH AND ORISHA: The Seven African Powers. Retrieved March 5, 2020, from wanderling.tripod.com website: http://wanderling.tripod.com/seven_powers.html

Tindall, D. (1998, November 1). Orisha Trinidad: Drums and Colours. Retrieved March 5, 2020, from Caribbean Beat Magazine website: https://www.caribbean-beat.com/issue-34/drums-and-colours#axzz6EgDG9SMm

Tobago Festivals. (2015, May 15). About. Retrieved March 5, 2020, from Tobago Heritage Festival website: https://www.tobagoheritagefestival.com/about/

Traditional Mas Archive. (2014). Moko Jumbie | Traditional Mas Archive. Retrieved March 5, 2020, from Traditionalmas.com website: https://www.traditionalmas.com/project/moko-jumbie/

WEST AFRICAN GOD AND GODDESS (2). (2012, August 25). Retrieved March 5, 2020, from WEST AFRICAN GOD AND GODDESS (2) website: https://kwekudee-tripdownmemorylane.blogspot.com/2012/08/sculptured-impression-of-olorun-1_25.html

Wigington, P. (2019a, February 13). What is the Santeria Religion? Retrieved March 5, 2020, from Learn Religions website: https://www.learnreligions.com/about-santeria-traditions-2562543

Wigington, P. (2019b, November 29). Yoruba Religion: History and Beliefs. Retrieved March 5, 2020, from Learn Religions website: https://www.learnreligions.com/yoruba-religion-4777660

About the Author

Monique Joiner Siedlak is a writer, witch, and warrior on a mission to awaken people to their greatest potential through the power of storytelling infused with mysticism, modern paganism, and new age spirituality. At the young age of 12, she began rigorously studying the fascinating philosophy of Wicca. By the time she was 20, she was self-initiated into the craft, and hasn't looked back ever since. To this day, she has authored over 40 books pertaining to the magick and mysteries of life.

To find out more about Monique Joiner Siedlak artistically, spiritually, and personally, feel free to visit her **official website**.

www.mojosiedlak.com

facebook.com/mojosiedlak

twitter.com/mojosiedlak

instagram.com/mojosiedlak

pinterest.com/mojosiedlak

bookbub.com/authors/monique-joiner-siedlak

More Books by Monique Joiner Siedlak

Practical Magick
Wiccan Basics
Candle Magick
Wiccan Spells
Love Spells
Abundance Spells
Herb Magick
Moon Magick
Creating Your Own Spells
Gypsy Magic
Protection Magick
Celtic Magick

Personal Growth and Development
Creative Visualization
Astral Projection for Beginners
Meditation for Beginners
Reiki for Beginners
Manifesting With the Law of Attraction
Stress Management
Being an Empath Today

The Yoga Collective
Yoga for Beginners
Yoga for Stress
Yoga for Back Pain
Yoga for Weight Loss
Yoga for Flexibility
Yoga for Advanced Beginners
Yoga for Fitness
Yoga for Runners
Yoga for Energy
Yoga for Your Sex Life
Yoga To Beat Depression and Anxiety
Yoga for Menstruation
Yoga to Detox Your Body
Yoga to Tone Your Body

A Natural Beautiful You
Creating Your Own Body Butter
Creating Your Own Body Scrub
Creating Your Own Body Spray

THANK YOU FOR READING MY BOOK! I REALLY APPRECIATE ALL OF YOUR FEEDBACK AND I LOVE TO HEAR WHAT YOU HAVE TO SAY. PLEASE LEAVE YOUR REVIEW AT YOUR FAVORITE RETAILER!